Picking Up

the Pieces to

100 Broken Promises

Part I

Picking Up the Pieces

to

100 Broken Promises

Part I

Yushima Cherry Burks

TAMARiND HiLL
.PRESS

THANK YOU

I am humbled and grateful that you have purchased and are reading my book. This book isn't just about me, it's about everyone who has faced trauma and who is seeking to come through on the other side, healed and whole. To me, it is more than a book. It's a glimpse inside of my inner most being. It's my family and friends, past and present, and you have decided to become a part of it. Thank you.

You can show your continued support by leaving a review and telling your friends and loved ones where *Picking Up the Pieces to 100 Broken Promises* can be purchased. Better yet, buying them a copy and giving them as gifts would be greatly appreciated. Give them the gift of the guide to healing; it is priceless.

Leaving a thoughtful review is the gift that keeps on giving. It provides me the opportunity to become a better writer, and it introduces me to those who haven't heard of me yet. Your review may be the one that reaches someone who needs to read this as much as I needed to write it. It can be short and sweet, "Wow, great read!" or more detailed, "Picking Up the Pieces to 100 Broken Promises has changed my life for the better. I saw myself in these pages and I recognized that healing is available for me too. I am so glad that I read this book. I will be buying this as gifts for my loved ones." Okay, so that last review was a bit much, but it's my hope that it reaches you all this much.

Let us keep the conversation going...

Keep in touch and get to know Yushima Cherry Burks better by visiting her website:

www.yearofyushima.com

Follow Yushima:

Instagram – @yearofyushima

Twitter – @yearofyushima

Youtube – Yushima Cherry

To every broken promise, heartache, pain, lie, disappointment and moment of despair; without you, I would have never learned how to allow God to put me back together again.

Table of Contents

FOREWORD

In order to find one's true self, many will have to find the strength to endure the journey that leads us to authentic healing. I have watched you grow and become this tenacious healer of people, even to the point of almost losing yourself in many sad and happy moments. I have been amazed that you could literally turn the other cheek and make it all seem worth the fight even when everyone else had given up. It was in middle of a Walmart conversation (as we would often find each other), I realized that only someone chosen by God could endure this unpredictable path you call life.

As I read through these pages filled with your most private yet revealing life seasons, I have much more understanding of who you are and why you are the strong woman you have become. Your penned memoir, "Picking Up the Pieces to 100 Broken Promises, Part I" encompasses a journey that many will identify with but have been too afraid to think or speak of. Readers will experience how the breaking of a promise can almost destroy a life in one instance and yet open up the door to healing in another circumstance. Congratulations Yushima and thank you for having the courage to use those 100 broken promises as the steppingstones to many more great moments for you and your readers.

Vonda Morrissette, MA
Licensed Professional Counselor
Choice One Counseling Services

PREFACE

I wrote this book to heal the little girl in me. She needed to know that through all of the pain and disappointment, life will get better.

In my journey to answer the question, "Who am I?" I found that all of my titles involved being something to someone else. That being: I am; a daughter, a mother, a wife, a friend, someone's enemy, a sister, a therapist etc. I've been many things to many people, but this process has helped me to focus on who I am as, by, and for myself. It helped me to identify what I have survived and how it has made me become who I am just as Yushima. Granted, I will always be something to someone else, but this journey has helped me understand that I am far more than what I am to and can do for others.

Through this process, I have learned to take better care of me. I have invested time in the little girl in me who needed me the most. Together we have healed from some things and together we are working on healing from others. I understand now that it is okay to put myself first, no matter how hard it is.

I am more than a burden bearer. I am a writer and a storyteller. I am a survivor and a lover of peace. I am unapologetically broken in some areas and healed in others. I am an anomaly. The things that occurred at the lowest points of my life in no way define me.

This book is not just for me. I want my readers to understand that while we may go through abuse, neglect, divorce, disappointment, abandonment, rape, loss, and make bad choices, there is hope. Healing is possible and you can get to the other side. On my new journey, I make promises to myself and keep them. Every waking day is a new day to work on myself.

Yushima Cherry Burks
Yushima Cherry Burks
2020

ACKNOWLEDGEMENT

Thank you would not be enough to say to God who has been there with me every step of the way, holding my hand through it all; to Him I am eternally grateful. It is because of Him and the promises He's made and kept that this book is possible. I am grateful to the journey that we are on and know that He'll always be with me.

Despite the challenges I have had in life, the lessons I've learned and the growth I've had would not have been possible without them. I am who I am because of my journey and I am grateful to everyone who's played a role in my growth.

To my dad, who will never get to read these pages, although so many are about him. To my children, I love you; and if I have ever broken a promise to you, may I have enough time to mend your hearts. To my husband, who loved me in spite of my broken parts, thank you. To my current friends, my past friends and my never friends, thank you for whatever role you were placed in my life to play.

INTRODUCTION

I've always loved writing, and from a very young age I've kept journals. In my later years and in my attempt to heal, I've used my journal entries more for reflection and investigation of myself and my life experiences. Recording what and how things happen in my life gave me the chance to look back and try to understand their impact better. This book is a collection of some of my journal entries that have helped me to understand why things happen and work on coming out on the other side, not unscathed, but as intact as possible.

When I took a personal inventory of the worst experiences in my life, I learned a lesson that shook me to the core. I am responsible for the things that I went through. Many of the heartache and pain were the direct result of one or two decisions that I made. In the instances where I could not directly pinpoint where my pain originated, I learned that I am still responsible for healing that too. The good news is that I am not alone. I have a relationship with God and He has never left my side. He went through hell with me and will continue to walk with and guide me.

People lie for all sorts of reasons. I have never met anyone that hasn't told a lie, myself included. Nothing justifies it but people do it anyway. Some people lie to spare the feelings of loved ones. If there is nothing to fear, there is no reason to lie and no matter how much we try to convince ourselves, all lies are bad. There is no such thing as a white lie; if the truth hurts, then a lie kills.

For every lie we've been told, God has a promise that we can actually stand on. This book is full of accounts of broken promises, lies and deception. Some of them are humorous, some tug at the heart strings, others are just outlandish; but one thing they all have in common is that they hurt the ones who have been lied to. They are told by and to those we love, including to ourselves.

Each broken promise in this book also has a promise from God. He is not a man that He should lie, and when you believe His promises to heal, love, comfort, protect and provide, everything in life will drastically change for the better. The focus shifts from depending on others for happiness, joy and peace; to allowing God to give you peace, joy, love and happiness. Love does not disappoint us, people do. People cannot heal us, that's God's job.

Being lied to by those that we love weakens years of trust, and though apologies may be given and accepted, I think it's safe to say that things never quite go back to being the same. In fact, it really doesn't matter who tells the lie: husbands, wives, boyfriends and girlfriends, parents, family members, friends, strangers and even a lie from a politician, can leave a nasty taste in our mouth. They are broken promises that break up families, tear down relationships, and destroy friendships. Luckily there is hope. Relationships can be restored, and trust can be rebuilt. The key lies within the one who has been hurt. It's not just about being the bigger person; it's about being a healed and complete person. It's deeper than we think. Unresolved feelings can turn into bitterness and resentment if un-forgiveness lingers in our heart.

Coming to terms with the possibility that the one that

hurt us may never apologize, or feel true remorse, makes the healing process that much easier. If forgiveness depended on the offender, it would only cause more pain since the one that offended often moves on in life, without thinking twice about the offense they committed. Forgiveness is for the one who has been hurt. It releases the power that the offender has on the offended.

Some give sincere apologies. They may realize the hurt they have caused and turn over a new leaf. They may right the wrongs they've committed, and swear to be honest at all costs. If this is the case, great! Count your blessings and move on. In some cases you will find that the offender apologizes only after getting caught; this is, more times than not, lip service. It's important to keep in mind that forgiveness is not contingent upon an apology, nor does it have anything to do with the other person. Forgiveness is for you.

Disappointment can build character, but it can also be discouraging and it is important to accept people for who they are. It is not necessary to remain in relationships with those who constantly make the choice to hurt you and misrepresent themselves. However, it is necessary to understand that their decision to be dishonest has nothing to do with you and it's not your job to "fix" them. Lies and deception are dangerous; otherwise rational people have killed in fits of rage as a result, only leaving them to regret their actions later. We must own our reactions and our actions; as we cannot control the actions of another. Decide to be a lover of truth; to tell the truth and accept being told the truth.

The layout of this book is such that the lessons I have learned along the way all have a story or part of my life attached to them. Some stories have more than one lessons and I have had to go through similar things at different points in my life experiencing the same kind of pain more than once. Upon reflection, I have learned that my experiences were more than just pain points and I have tried to communicate this in a way that you understand that; for everything in our lives, God has a promise that we can stand on and He keeps His promises.

His Promise

And you will know the truth, and the truth will set you free.

- John 8:32

My Promise

I promise to forgive and give grace to those who hurt me and to myself when I fall short of my own expectations.

CHAPTER 1

The Foundation I was

Built On

The process of writing is cathartic for me. I began writing this collection of events in my journal in my mid-twenties because I needed closure, but when one chapter finished, another one opened and the story continued. I soon realized that as it was helping me to deal with one issue, it paved the way to face another. When my ex-husband, left, I needed to be in control of something and I knew that I could make sense of it all once I put it on paper. I needed to release it from my mind, my space and my thoughts. I needed to see change. I felt stuck, not because I still wanted to be with him, but because I needed to start over and I had no idea how I was going to do that. Writing my day-to-day experiences helped me to see the progression that I was making. It also paved the way for me to look deeper at everything else that had happened up to being abandoned by my ex-husband.

I had to start creating *Picking Up The Pieces of 100 Broken Promises, Part I* while I was still in the process of healing. If I had waited until I was fully healed, this book would still be incomplete. I was going through a very difficult time in my life and experiencing the effects of grief, abandonment and hopelessness. I found out later, that this is the perfect state to be in for God to do His perfect work. He removed all of my dependencies, including a husband that I shouldn't have married in the first place. This book helped me to process all that was happening to me and with me. It's raw and real, some parts are embarrassing, others make me proud; it's a process, and it's all real.

I found out that my now ex-husband (let's call him, Mitch) had been living a double life. He lead me to believe that he was out of state working as a tattoo artist and for two months, he visited and made excuses for leaving for weeks at a time. I knew something was up, but I couldn't put my finger on it. Finally, on his last visit, the Holy Spirit showed me exactly what he was doing. He was living with another woman in Georgia. He had lied to her saying that I left him and that we were in the process of a divorce. There was no way for me to know this and when I blurted it out, I was just as surprised as he was. He ran out of the house and made a few phone calls, only to come back and try to pry out of me where I had gotten that information from.

Mitch had just left me in a new state, jobless, an undergrad and with a three year-old son who adored him so much that he wouldn't sleep until he came home. This abandonment threatened to destroy my son. Mitch wouldn't return my calls, I knew the marriage was over, but I needed him to be a father. I put our son in therapy, and began trying to rebuild my life that was built on 100 broken promises. I needed a new foundation, because the one that I had depended on was all but dependable.

His Promise

For there is nothing hidden that will not be disclosed, and nothing concealed that will not be known or brought out into the open.

- Luke 8:17

My Promise

I promise to listen when the Holy Spirit talks to me instead of trying to convince God to allow me to have my way, obviously my picker is broken.

Fool's Gold

One of the most painful truths I discovered was that the love I felt and wanted so badly, was not love at all. For every truth God gives, satan has a counterfeit. The truth is, I should have never expected someone who did not have a relationship with God to love me. That was foolish, but so was I. I thought that love was something fluid; sometimes it was good, and sometimes it was bad. I thought that love hurts, and I always had to be the one to "fix" it when it went left.

From a young age, I was taught that love came in different forms. My dad taught me that God is love. He showed me by loving me and being gentle and kind. He was my protector, my provider and my best friend. I talked to him about everything. If he didn't approve of my choices, he let me know, but always did it in love. My mother, on the other hand, taught me that love is pain. I had to earn her love. I was abused physically and verbally until I was twenty-six years old. Yes, twenty-six years old. I had two kids and a husband and I was still a scared five-year-old around my mother. It wasn't until a friend of mine witnessed her abuse and jumped between us that I realized this was wrong. The irony was that, by this time, I was an advocate against child abuse and neglect.

When I was eight years old, the first person who molested me was my brother's friend. He would whisper in my ear that he loved me. I couldn't imagine telling my mother, as I was sure I would be blamed. I was blamed for her abusive ways toward me so I didn't expect anything else. I didn't even consider telling my father. He loved me, but he left me there, so I felt in some ways that I deserved it. My idea of love was warped from its foundation; no wonder I made the decisions I did. My father loved me but he left, so love wasn't always good.

The guys that I dated wanted me to show them love, which always required a sacrifice of some sort. I sacrificed my morals, time, friends, my youth, innocence and common sense and had I died in that sin, my salvation. There were a few that did not expect me to have sex with them. Not everyone who wanted me, got me, but more got me than I wanted. I was a mess trying to sift through lust, greed and pain to find love.

Looking back on this aspect of my life there is one thing I know now that I did not know then. Love only wants what's best for me. It is concerned about my well-being, including my salvation. As an adult, I can recognize what love is and what it isn't. I know that someone who continually hurts me, does not love me. That does not mean that someone who loves me, will not hurt me. Once I agree to love, hurt is sure to follow, but it will not stay there, and it will not be intentional.

His Promise

Love is patient. Love is kind. It does not want what belongs to others. It does not brag. It is not proud. It is not rude. It does not look out for its own interests. It does not easily become angry. It does not keep track of other people's wrongs. Love is not happy with evil. But it is full of joy when the truth is spoken. It always protects. It always trusts. It always hopes. It never gives up. Love never fails.

\- 1 Corinthians 13:4-8

My Promise

I promise to accept love in all of its forms, from life lessons to healing and everything in between. Abuse is not love, but loving myself in spite of the abuse is my goal.

Reckless Behaviour

The saying, "Whatever doesn't kill you, makes you stronger," cannot be applied in some situations; like abuse for instance. Going through a childhood laced with abuse, divorce and at times neglect, did not make me stronger. It made me insecure, unsure and afraid. I grew up thinking that everyone that loved me would abuse me and everyone that I loved would leave me. I was pretty messed up.

Issues from my past distorted my pallet for understanding what is acceptable and unacceptable. When these issues were brought up in the pursuit of healing, it was an anomaly how my mom said that she did not remember the horror she put me through. She said she did the best that she could and "If you know better, you do better." I would have been able to accept this had she not known better. She knew better; she showed my brother love and concern. She attended his football games and encouraged him to make friends.

With me on the other hand, she wasn't that great of a mother. She tried to beat the creativity out of me and called me every name in the book except a child of God. I grew up thinking that I was nothing, worthy of nothing and destined to be nothing. Even with the love and encouragement my father gave me, it was difficult being surrounded by hate and negativity on a daily basis. When my father moved from Wisconsin to Alabama, the abuse got worse and there was no one to cover me from the wrath of my mother.

So, when I eventually went through my own divorce I was hypervigilant in trying to make the transition as painless as possible for my own son Mikey, he was only two years old. I had to hold it together, continue to nurture, love and support him, and figure out our new normal. I had to be the better parent because I did not want to put my child through what I went through. Without a doubt, I was going to do everything I could to make sure that my child was not going to feel the way my mother made me feel as an adult.

Working in my field, social work, I have heard it all. "You are fine, the past does not matter," said one abusive mother to the only child of hers that continues to talk to her. I've witnessed the alcoholic dad who does not remember the beatings his wife and children suffered for years. There are a million scenarios that fall under abuse.

I'm not sure my mother forsook me but I know now that she was hurt and hurt people hurt people. I can only imagine the things that my own kids tell their therapists. No matter how much we want to protect and love our children, we will inflict some trauma without knowing it. I just hope they will love me anyway and that I will be forgiven for the mistakes I make with them.

Some parents who feel that they are different now feel like the children who were abused should forgive and forget. In order for the victim/survivor to receive healing, the abuser must be forgiven; the forgotten part is where the lines are blurred. Forgiving does not mean putting myself in the position to continually be abused in any fashion. I believe that it is necessary for adult survivors of abuse to receive help, whatever help they feel will work, professional or not. It helps to talk about it, pray about it and make a conscious decision to be happy, healthy and whole. While time does not heal any wounds, God has a promise that is timeless.

His Promise

I will give you back your health and heal your wounds.

-   Jeremiah 30:17

My Promise

I promise not to allow my past trauma to continue to dominate the narrative in my mind.

Making New Memories

I wish I could remember more about my childhood. It's all so black and white. I remember my mother wanting me to look nice, I always had to look put together. I would have the nicest clothes to cover my bruises. My hair was long enough to shield black eyes or bruised cheeks. I wish I could have enjoyed the outfits she took so much time to put together for me. I wish I could have enjoyed her more. I wish she could have enjoyed me. There is so much pain and shame in these memories. Even now, I wonder what she would think of me for writing my truth, exposing hers. Although I am writing about it, I have forgiven my mother and I love her very much.

There are so many black holes of missing memories but I remember our family outings and pizza Friday's. We went to Chuck E. Cheese at least once a month. I remember riding my bike outside and sharing roller skates with my friend across the street. I remember my dad doing my hair, and my pigtails always being uneven, but I was so proud of them, because he took his time to do them. I remember my mother taking me to get my hair done professionally, and that was her contribution to making me pretty.

I want to remember the good so badly, to find something that I can hold on to about my mother during that time. I do remember her laugh, it was hearty. She laughed unabashedly, with her mouth open, and she would throw her head back. She was very beautiful to me. She reminded me of Claire Huxtable from The Cosby Show. She wore her hair feathered and it moved whenever she did. I loved her. I still love her, I just wish I could remember more.

I had this conversation with her a while ago, once I had begun the process of forgiving her, where I asked her to tell me some good things about my childhood that she could remember. She said that it couldn't have been all bad, but she couldn't remember anything good herself. That was alarming for me.

I always wanted to please my mother. As I got older and I reached out to her, I made it a point to create memories that I could share with my children that wouldn't give them nightmares. I invited her to places like the zoo and the museum with me. I invited her to my home and I visited her often. When she needed her space, I gave it to her and when I needed mine, I took it. I have always wanted to have a healthy mother-daughter relationship with my mother.

The love from my father and the values he instilled in me has always allowed me to keep trying with my mother. Whenever I called my dad to get advice or vent, he would never speak badly about her. He would quote the same Scripture, every time and it has been with his influence that I am able to forgive and still love my mother. I am so grateful for having a foundation built on the Word of God, without it, I would not have anything to hold on to.

His Promise

When my father and my mother forsake me, then the Lord will take me up.

- Psalms 27:10

My Promise

I promise to accept what I can and cannot change.

Dead Inside

When I think about restoration, I think about all of the nights that I prayed for death and all of the mornings I cursed life. I knew God, I knew of God. I didn't have my own relationship with Him, yet. I wanted to be zealous like my father about how good He was, and I didn't doubt it, but I didn't understand it either. The concept of unconditional love wasn't lost on me, because I still loved my mother. I was a scared, lonely teenager and I knew God loved me, because my dad loved me with all my flaws, just as I was, but it wasn't enough.

There was nothing sweet about my sixteenth birthday. I was severely depressed and desperate for attention. My dad was in Alabama and I lived with my mother. I had sex with my boyfriend just to feel something other than pain, but the results of that ended up being more pain than I could ever imagine. I ended up pregnant. I couldn't hide it from my mom. I didn't know it at the time, but my severe morning sickness that lasted all day was much more than morning sickness. It was a life threatening illness that occurs during pregnancy called hyperemesis gravidarum, I would have suffered through this with every pregnancy. I was four and a half months when my mother took me to get an abortion. I had already felt the baby kick and the ultrasound showed that he was a boy. There was nothing that I could do to get over the pain of killing my baby.

Shortly after the abortion, my mother called my father to come and get me, and as always, he was there within twenty-four hours. He told her that he wished she had called sooner, before she made the choice to abort the baby, and he would have picked me up then.

I can't remember the drive back to Alabama or how long it was before I attempted suicide. I remember a deep gut wrenching pang in my heart that nothing could fill. My father prayed with me and for me every day. He called off work often so that I wouldn't be home alone. He sat in the bed with me and sung to me. He rocked me in his arms as if I were a toddler again. None of that lessened my pain, or maybe it did, but my pain was so deep that I didn't recognize any improvement.

The day I took the pills, I wanted to die peacefully in my sleep. I took twenty-three extra strength Tylenol. Who knew that that was not enough to cause an imminent death? I did find out that I was allergic to codeine and ended up calling my father six hours later and telling him what I had done. Instead of dying, I felt really sick and I vomited most of the pills out anyway.

My father rushed me to the hospital, where I was greeted by an annoyed doctor and sarcastic nurses who taunted me for my "foolish" action. I remember being forced to take charcoal and being threatened with a stomach pump. The doctor was very graphic about how painful it would be and how sore my throat would be after the procedure.

My father was in the hallway for what seemed like hours pleading with my mother to talk to me. I shook my head profusely as he walked toward me, with his arm outstretched to hand me the phone. I refused to grab it, but he placed it up to my ear anyway. She very quietly began to speak, "You dumb bitch. You can't even kill yourself right. The next time you want to die, slit your wrists and sit in the tub, or take more pills and lay your ass down. You don't call somebody to come rescue you. You can't even die right."

I looked up at my dad, indicating that our conversation was over, and he smiled, hoping that this was the incident that would bring my mother to her senses, and help us move on. It would be sixteen more years before I told him what she said to me that day.

I wish I could say that this would be the last time I experienced any of these things, but it wasn't. I ended up pregnant with my daughter a year later, my father did pick me up and she was born beautiful and healthy. My struggle with depression did not end there, nor did my attempts at suicide. I just thank God that He had other plans for me and that my end did not come when I wanted it to.

Having an abortion is a decision that millions of women and families make and while some think it's taking the easy way out, it's a decision that has lasting effects. I believe a lot of my choices after the abortion were to punish myself. It took years, but I have finally forgiven myself. I no longer blame my mother for doing what she thought was best for me. I forgave my ex-boyfriend for not being capable of being there, hell I couldn't be there for myself, what did I expect from a sixteen year old boy?

His Promise

For I know the plans I have for you, declares the Lord, plans for welfare and not for evil, to give you a future and a hope.

- Jeremiah 29:11

My Promise

I promise to stand in my truth, no matter how painful it may be.

Knee Deep

As a teenager, I struggled with depression. It was this sadness that caused me to put myself in situations that could have cost me my life. I can't remember why I felt utterly despondent that day. It was different from the other days. I know that the night before, my mother was in a mood, so that meant I got it. I remember waking up sick to my stomach that I had to face another day.

One of the many times I skipped school, I accepted a ride from a stranger. Once I accepted the ride, he very calmly told me that we were driving up to the hotel down the street. I didn't object. I didn't run or jump out of the car. I wasn't even scared. It's like part of me welcomed death, the other part of me just wanted my mother to find my blooded half-dead body in a hotel room just so I could hear her whisper, "I'm sorry" or "I love you." I was hurt and the only thing that I attracted was more pain.

Once we arrived at the hotel room, I waited for him to hurt me. I watched him intently, as he tried to engage me in a conversation about school and the weather as if we were old friends. His hair was greasy and curly, he wore a pressed white button down shirt, tight blue jeans with a large round belt buckle, and cowboy boots. All I could think was that I rarely saw Black men wear cowboy boots.

He asked me my age and I told him sixteen; he told me he was thirty-two. At the time, that seemed so old to me and I remember thinking how gross he was for wanting to have sex with a teenager. I felt dirty when he began complimenting me. It wasn't until he began undressing that I felt uncomfortable. It was late for common sense to kick in. I had avoided it all of this time. Now he stood between me and the door. I sat quietly on the bed.

I wasn't a virgin, but I had never done anything like this. I only had a couple of boyfriends in my life and this was way out of character for me. I wanted to leave, and when I stood up, he forcefully held my arm and directed me back to the bed. I insisted that he put on a condom, he commented on how that was a good decision. He went on to say that I should always suggest that any boy I sleep with puts on a condom. I felt like I was getting life lessons from a man that was about to rape me. The story of my life.

When it was over, he made a telephone call from his huge flip phone. He was late picking up his wife from work. He sounded so apologetic on the call. He knew what to say to calm her. He promised her that he would be there shortly, he had been "held up" and he ended the call with, "I love you."

He put his clothes on and walked out of the door. Looking back, he told me I could have the room for one more hour if I wanted it, but I had to be out by twelve. He only paid for three hours. Once he drove off, I walked back to school and stayed for the rest of the day as if nothing happened. Instead of telling someone what happened to me, I thought about how good I was at hiding my pain. I was almost proud of it. No. I was proud of it. I had become a master of disguise.

Who was I fooling? No one. I was a sixteen year old mess. I really felt like I had gotten away with something that day. My behaviour was a textbook cry for help. If one person had asked me if I was okay, I would have had a full come apart. I was dying for attention, any kind of attention. I was still reeling from the abortion that I had and I didn't know how to forgive myself at this point. I was also angry, I was angry at everyone for not noticing my pain and I was angry at myself for being in pain.

Looking back, I wished I had spoken to a school counsellor or to one of my friends' moms. Things may have been different. Being sixteen was hard and I didn't have the internet with millions of doctored images and opinions to sift through on a daily basis. Parents, talk to your teenagers, be a listening ear, give them good advice and allow them to express themselves, you just may save their life.

His Promise

Heal me, O Lord, and I shall be healed; save me, and I shall be saved, for you are my praise.

- Jeremiah 17:14

My Promise

I promise to ask for help when I need it. I know that I do not have to suffer alone.

Twinkie Twinkie Little Star

One friendship that I will always miss is my dear friend, Twinkie. Twinkie was cute as button. She smiled all of the time and was friendly with everyone. All of the girls wanted to be like her and all of the guys wanted her. We were thick as thieves for years. I had a crush on her brother, but I ended up meeting her and we were fast friends.

Twinkie lived three houses down, in the corner house. I was fourteen and she was seventeen. She was the one I called when my mother got "out of control" and I needed to talk. Twinkie's mom was very strict, so she couldn't come by when her mother was home, because I had an older brother. Twinkie wasn't thinking about Curtis, but we couldn't convince her mother of that.

Twinkie trained every day to be an American Gladiator. They were coming to Milwaukee, and Twinkie was going to try out. She would have made it too, but she got pregnant by her high-school sweetheart. Being a teen mom did not stop her graduating top of her class, while holding down two jobs. She handled her business and I admired her for that.

She knew everything about me. She was one of the few friends who actually witnessed my mother's angst against me. While I stood at least five inches taller than her, she became my protector. Twinkie knew that if she came over, my mother would not be as abusive as she normally was. When things got too out of hand at home, her house was the one I went to for respite. When I ran away, I went to her house, but that was short lived, since my mom called threatening her mother with harbouring a runaway.

At seventeen when I got pregnant with my daughter, I moved to Alabama. When my daughter was born, naturally, I named her after Twinkie. Twinkie was the reason for my dad's five hundred dollar telephone bill. My dad was kind enough to drive me to Milwaukee to be there for the birth of Twinkie's first baby boy. When I moved back to Milwaukee, we picked up where we left off. By that time, she had married her high-school sweetheart and had another boy. Unfortunately, her husband was a great provider and a wonderful father, but a horrible husband. He cheated and lied, and eventually Twinkie left him. I was there for her during this time, like she had been there for me.

Twinkie and I remained friends well into our late twenties. We lived together at different points in our lives. We shared moments that no one but God witnessed. I would still call her a friend today, but now it's awkward. I think things changed when she became involved with her cousin's long-time boyfriend. Her cousin had three kids with Chubby, and she loved him, but Twinkie snagged him and they moved in together. I guess when you put someone on a pedestal, especially when they didn't ask to be there, the fall is hard.

I loved Twinkie, but I could not support what she had done to her cousin. I began to worry about our relationship. I wondered if she would ever betray me. I couldn't imagine it, but I still worried about it. Chubby and Twinkie stayed together for about five years on and off. I visited them, but not often. Eventually, I got married and moved on with my life. We spoke here and there, but things weren't the same.

I know that we have a history and I hope that one day

Twinkie and I will come back together and be as close as we once were. I know what it's like to hurt and make decisions based on emotions. I am not holding any grudges against Twinkie, in fact, if I still lived in Milwaukee, I think we would still be very close. I also know that she is human and I need to remember not to judge people based on the idea of them that I have in my head, but on their own merit. I am not saying that I shouldn't have a standard or that I shouldn't set boundaries. What I am saying is that I am learning to accept people for who they are, the good and the bad; and looking back, Twinkie's good outweighed her bad.

His Promise

Be kind to one another, tenderhearted, forgiving one another, as God in Christ forgave you.

-   Ephesians 4:32

My Promise

I promise to be open and available for a loved one that is in pain.

CHAPTER 2

Parenting

I Chose You

My decision to be a teen mother was a selfish and immature one. At the time, I wanted to believe that I was doing the mature thing, but the reality was that I was really being selfish. I did not consider the amount of work that it took to be a parent, so I couldn't have known what my parents were going through. I put my parents through unneeded stress. My dad worked two full-time jobs to take care of us.

Once I was on my own, I understood what it meant to be the only source of support for my child. That was a great duty for an eighteen year-old and an even greater burden for a one year-old. I wanted AJ, because I loved her. My love did not prevent her from getting hurt, it did not supply her with food, water or shelter, it did not keep her from hating me. My love, my intention, my hope for her and my desire to be supermom was anything but.

Love was not all that I needed, I needed maturity, I needed experience, I needed my mother, I needed her father, I needed family, I needed a better paying job, an education, a car, support, my own home, but most of all I needed God. My relationship with God had not developed enough for me to call on Him like my dad always suggested I do. I prayed, I went to church, but I had not yet learned to trust Him. I was presumptuous to think that I could do it on my own. I was selfish to want a baby that I could not take care of without great sacrifice. I was foolish to believe that I was in any condition to love her enough. I was broken, and a broken person makes a broken parent. I had not yet healed from the rejection, hurt and pain that I had suffered. My brain wasn't finished developing, but I was in charge of helping a beautiful innocent human being develop.

I was a child. I may have been more mature than most. I did the very best I could and even then, I did better than I thought I should, but I was a teenager. I was full of doubt. I acted stronger than I was. I wish I knew what I thought I did. I became the best mother that I could, but I was still a teenager. I did not do drugs, I did not drink, I did not party and go to clubs like my friends. I watched Sesame Street, Bananas in Pajamas and Barney excessively. I stayed home with her. I sang to her. I read books to her.

I taught her the alphabet and her numbers.

I prayed with her every day and every night. I took her to the park, we went on long walks and I talked to her. We went to the zoo and the museum. I cooked three meals a day for her. I made the best out of what we had. I made playdates for her and I stayed with her. I loved her, but I was just a broken child and that always finds a way to seep out and cause unwarranted pain.

If I had waited to have AJ, I would never have had her, so I don't regret having her, but I still cringe at the thought of me not being enough for her. I still hurt at the thought of the life I could not give her. I thank God that we made it; though we are not unscathed, we made it. I still can't help but wonder what her life would have been like if I had more to give.

His Promise

Here for the third time I am ready to come to you. And I will not be a burden, for I seek not what is yours but you. For children are not obligated to save up for their parents, but parents for their children.

- 2 Corinthians 12:14

My Promise

I promise to put my needs ahead of my wants, especially when it impacts others.

Parental Rejection

As a mother, I have always wanted to protect my children from the things I faced in my childhood. One of those many things is having to deal with the lack of a sense of belonging. I want my children to know that they are loved and wanted. I want them to know that they are special and to never feel worthless or rejected. Unfortunately, I had to learn that it doesn't end with me.

The moment I found out that I was pregnant with AJ, I knew that I had to leave Wisconsin, or she would never have been born. My mom wanted me to have an abortion and as usual, my dad came to the rescue. AJ was born in Alabama, and my dad was great for her. We made a family out of my closest friends and we loved her so much. I had never experienced a love like that. Being a teen mom, I was often confronted with dilemmas surrounding AJ's real family. I wanted her to know her father's family. He lived with his aunt and she was stern, but we never really had a heart to heart. I did write a few letters informing them about AJ's birth, but I never heard back from them.

We moved back to Wisconsin when AJ was about one year old. I contacted her father again, and he agreed to meet me at the mall. I was surprised when he came. I was ecstatic when he picked her up from her stroller and cradled her like the daughter he had always wanted. Being the dreamer that I am, I thought that he would be there for her. I was wrong. That was the last time I saw him until she turned eight years old. If I had been patient and wiser, I would not have had premarital sex, and I would not had been a teenage mom stalking her daughter's father. It was harder back then, there wasn't internet to do the work for me, I had to become a real sleuth.

When AJ was eight years old, I found Bo online and gave him a call. He actually sounded relieved and asked if I could pick him up from Green Bay, Wisconsin. It was about an hour and a half away, but I wanted him to meet AJ so I did. All contact that they had from that point on was because of his girlfriend. She did most of the shopping for AJ, answered my calls and allowed AJ to get to know her little brother, Jacob. I was grateful for this time, I had never seen AJ so happy. I felt complete, but it was short lived. Bo soon went back to his elusive ways and AJ suffered yet again. I could not have been more disappointed in myself.

I had finally had enough. My daughter deserved to have a loving family. She needed this. I put my pride aside and prepared myself to meet with Bo's aunt. She had not moved and I was ready to help cultivate the family AJ never had. I knew I would not be enough for her, and she needed someone; hell, I needed someone.

I walked up the infamous red stairs, my palms were sweaty, I had rehearsed this moment over and over again. There was no time like now. My heart was in my chest. AJ was safe at school. I had all of the time in the world. I was ready. When I rang the doorbell, it took forever for Shirley to answer. When she opened the door, she recognized me, and she knew why I was there.

I can't remember if she had asked me in or not, but I knew that I was going to talk to her even if I had to stand outside in the cold November weather. I showed her a picture of AJ, and before I could say a word, she said, "Is that Bo's little girl?" I told her that it was and I went on to explain that I really wanted them to be a part of her life. She nodded while I spoke, not in agreeance, but in acknowledgement.

I gave her my contact information, but I never heard from her. I had considered contacting her again, but I'm not a fan of constant rejection. AJ is now twenty-four years old and she still wonders about them. I was never enough for her. I couldn't have been. That's why God created laws to prevent situations like these.

I wasn't designed to parent alone, neither was my mother, or her mother, or my father. We were designed to have two parents and to share the joy and the burden of raising children together. I see that now, and so does AJ. I could not provide a father for her. I could not give her what she needed. Even today, I am not enough, but I am thankful that I no longer have to be. I give my children to God daily and I pray that He fills the void that tugs at their hearts.

His Promise

Though my father and mother forsake me, the LORD will receive me.

- Psalms 27:10

My Promise

I promise to love that teenager that needed to be loved back then.

Parenting in Fear

The most important job that I have been given is parenthood. Fear has played a huge part in some of the decisions that I have made as a parent. I know what it's like to watch my children suffer at the hands of another, directly and indirectly. I have never felt so powerless in my life as I do as a parent.

Knowing that this world is set up systematically to ensure their failure has made me hypervigilant and it causes me to be in constant conflict with school officials, children services and everyone else who poses a threat to my children. It is not a task that I take lightly. I've made mistakes and I won't ignore them. Decisions that I have made are still impacting my children's lives. Being responsible for another human being engulfs my every waking moment. All of the love that I have in my heart did not stop me from being foolish at times, selfish at times and just plain stupid sometimes. I brought children into a world full of hatred, pain and suffering, and I can't protect them all of the time.

Raising AJ was difficult for me and her. I don't know any mother who chose to be a single parent. I know I didn't choose to raise a child without a father. I met the man of my dreams, we fell in love and we were going to live happily ever after. That was the story my seventeen-year-old self concocted. The truth was that I was in pain. I hated being at home. I felt lonely and alone. I craved love. My dad was miles away, and not even his love or wisdom comforted me during this time in my life.

I believed my boyfriend when he said that he couldn't have kids, and it would be okay. I didn't mind if I did get pregnant, this was the love of my life. Unfortunately, the news of a pregnancy was not in his top ten life goals and he let that be known. He was going to play in the NBA, like his cousin, and he did not want any part of this situation. I did not pursue him at that time, I just wanted my baby. I was young and dumb, but I knew that I couldn't make anyone love me or their child. I learned that from experience.

With Mikey, I knew in my heart that Mitch was not the one for me, but it was the closest thing to a family of my own that I had ever experienced. I was getting older, and having a baby at twenty-eight should have been easier. I was in a different place in my life. I had a great career. I was financially stable and I was married. It should have been a cinch. The thought of raising a baby with my husband was special to me. I loved his daughter like she was my own and with her and AJ being so close in age, it seemed like the right place to be. Still, I wondered if Mitch and I would grow old together. He did the best that he could with the girls. He didn't have the best example growing up and we both were winging it. With all of the cheating and the lying, a divorce was inevitable. I lost more than a husband, I lost a father for my three-year-old son, a step-dad for my daughter and I lost my step-daughter.

If someone had told me that I would have another child after I had Mikey, I would have rebuked them. After Mitch and I divorced, I didn't plan on having any more children. I knew I would eventually remarry, it was in my heart, but having another child wasn't in my plans. I am so glad God does not listen to my plans.

My third child, Jackson, was quite the surprise. Who

knew that the doctors were wrong when they said that I couldn't have any more children. I explained that I had heard this before seven years prior and yet I was still unable to get the tubal that I requested. He made his appearance shortly after I had lost about one hundred pounds. My husband, Quan, was happy about raising Jackson with his new wife. I was not looking forward to the symptoms of hyperemesis gravidarum that plagued my first two pregnancies. The end result was a healthy baby boy and I couldn't be happier with my little cuddle buddy.

Jack was born when Mikey was seven years old and AJ was seventeen. I started all the way over. I didn't know that I needed my little boy, Jack, until he was here. Jack is seven years old now. Raising my son Jack, with my husband of nine years, Quan, is a totally different experience for me. I am privy to seeing the development of a child who loves and adores his father.

Blending our families wasn't easy. I only had the privilege of meeting one of his children, and she is a blessing. She's beautiful and smart as ever. She is in college pursuing her dream career and I look forward to seeing the woman she becomes. She's always been respectful and loving.

Mikey and Quan's relationship didn't develop the way I thought it would, but it's not because Quan didn't try. When he and I married, Mikey was four years old and in the beginning he accepted and respected Quan. AJ was in Connecticut, so she didn't have an opinion one way or another.

When Mikey was young, Quan would get up in the middle of the night and give him breathing treatments, his asthma would flare up sometimes and Quan would get to him before I would wake up. Quan went to visit him at school and ate lunch with him. He took him to doctor's appointments and to get haircuts. He taught him how to ride his bike and how to handle bullies. He did everything I had hoped he would as a father to Mikey. When Jack was born, Mikey was not having it and things changed drastically with him. He started wanting his "own dad" and when I couldn't make that happen, things took a turn for the worse.

Once he got older, he started to rebel and he made it

known that he did not respect him as a father. Quan always introduced Mikey as his son, but Mikey corrected him and made it known that there was no relation between them. I pray that God will heal us all.

The circumstances surrounding my children are all different. I wish I had done things differently to make their lives easier now, but most of my life I have been barely hanging on. Hindsight is indeed 20/20. I pray daily that my kids make better decisions than I did. I know that GOD is the only One that can create life and I know that each child that grew in my womb was placed there and given life by the Creator and Architect of life itself. I hate to use the word regret, knowing that this may all work for His glory, so I won't.

His Promise

Children are a gift from the Lord, they are a reward from Him.

\-   Psalms 127:3

My Promise

I promise to love my children, without placing an expectation on their personal journey and growth.

CHAPTER 3
Experience, Forgiveness, Growth

Inconsiderate Yushima

In my early twenties, I met the sweetest person ever at work. I worked at a pharmaceutical company in the customer service department. She was about four foot eight and cute as a button. She was a few years older than me, but we had so much in common. We both had daughters. We both wanted to move to a better place. We were both newly single. Perfect roommate material.

Up until this point, I had never had a roommate. I always lived on my own, with my daughter and/or my daughter and my ex. My three year plan was up and I was ready to move out of public housing, or what we call "the projects." We made the plans, paid our deposits and moved in. Things were going well. We cooked for each other. We shared our food and our daughters got along great. It was a good situation to be in.

We had our differences, different religious beliefs; she was a Buddhist and I was a Christian. Actually, she was probably more faithful to her god than I was mine. The chanting was weird for me and I did feel a presence there that was not God, but other than that, I really enjoyed Stephanie. She was fun and outgoing, she danced and laughed with her mouth open like me.

Inevitably, we had begun dating guys. We were two fine young women, and we had begun dating friends. Her new beau happened to be married to a childhood friend of mine. We grew up in church together, but I had never met her husband. We saw each other every Sabbath at church. Months later, I found out, but I can't remember how. I think it was through her saying my name to him though – I have a very unusual middle name, Camoy.

Maybe I saw a picture of them together, either way, it came out. I had a decision to make. Of course I spoke to my roommate, after pleading with him to tell her himself. I gave him a certain amount of time to do it, before I told her. I didn't want to tell his wife, and destroy a marriage before giving them an opportunity to make it right.

My dear friend Stephanie was fresh out of a divorce, and she felt like his adulterous behaviour should not stop her fun. She eventually confronted him, but the affair lasted for a while. We talked about it. I knew at times she felt bad, since she had been cheated on by her husband.

I know what it's like to be comforted by more pain. I was young and unmarried, so I didn't feel like my opinion was that important. It really put me in an awkward position. Later when my childhood friend, Judy, found out, we talked about it. I am glad she did not hold it against me, because I did not have control over that grown man's behaviour. Judy then told me that my new boo, was engaged to be married. He tried it, but I couldn't deal with that.

After that dating fiasco, I met someone new. His name was Raymond. He was mature, had a great job, and loved his mother and his kids. He was older than me and we had so much fun together. Eventually, I wanted to spend more time with him. He came over just about every day. Stephanie was incredibly patient with me, but at the time I didn't appreciate it. I was being selfish. He was there a lot. I didn't consider her and I justified it by making him come by later when the kids were asleep. I should not have had him in the house that much regardless. I could have spent more time at his place.

There are a ton of things that I could have done differently. Like kept it simple, instead of immersing myself into his world. When my selfishness started to cause conflict, I told Stephanie that I wanted to break my lease six months early. I was ready to move out because I was in love and Raymond and I were getting married. I wished she would have just punched me in the face to wake me up right then. We came to a compromise so I could move out but our friendship was never the same.

This story is so embarrassing to me because I was so immature and selfish in this matter. Stephanie was a saint. I don't know how she put up with me. A few years ago, I unpacked a bin that I've had for years and I found her handheld blow dryer that she loaned me in it. I was the worst. I haven't spoken to her in years. Stephanie and I were in touch via social media years ago, but I took a hiatus from it and we lost touch. I wonder if I was her last roommate? I wish her well and I hope she forgives me for being such a brat. Sorry again, Stephanie.

I am so glad God has matured me and has given me wisdom to be a better person and a better friend. I hope I

live up to what is expected from a good friend with my girls
now.

His Promise

For wisdom is more precious than rubies, and nothing you desire can compare with her.

-       Proverbs 8:11

My Promise

I promise to be mindful of others.

Mighty Misha

In my early twenties, I ran into Misha, a childhood friend. Our parents knew each other before we were born. We were neighbours at one point and we played together every day while our parents hung out. Her mother made the best peach cobbler ever and it was always fun at her house. Except that time her father got drunk and picked me up by my ponytails. My father was not happy to hear about that and they did have a "talk" about it.

Having Misha around was refreshing. I loved the time we spent reminiscing and I could be myself around her. We talked about everything, from our parents, to what we wanted to do with our life. We laughed out loud and really enjoyed each-other's company. She did not have kids, but she didn't mind mentoring a family friend that was staying with me. Isabell moved in with me as a teenager. She wasn't getting along with her parents and I tried to mend that broken relationship, but it was not working out.

Misha and Isabell spent a lot of time together; they became close as sisters. It was great having them there together. I worked full-time, so during summer hours, they stayed at my house since Isabell did not have school. One night, Misha and Isabell wanted to borrow my car and I told them, no. I did not feel comfortable with that since I was responsible for Isabell. It was already nine o'clock, and I was tired. I was asleep by nine fifteen at the latest.

I received a call at two o'clock in the morning. Misha and Isabel had been in an accident and they hit a light pole. My car was totalled. They were both fine and they did not suffer any lasting injuries, but my car was not fine. Misha did not have a license and the city wanted to charge me for the damage she made to the light pole.

I had full coverage insurance, but it did not cover the damage in this accident. Sometimes life is like that. We can think that we have full coverage, and something happens that catches us completely off guard. I found out that in cases like this, I can always count on God to pick up the pieces all around me. I know Misha could not have known that this would happen. Sometimes we do things without considering the consequences.

Looking back, I don't know what I was thinking. I had

AJ and I also took on a full teenager while in my early twenties. I don't regret it, but I could have done some things differently. Although it was something that irked me because the car was a total loss, I am so happy that Misha and Isabell were okay after that accident. Isabell and I talk almost daily via social media. I haven't brought this up to her, but I wonder if she remembers.

I haven't heard from Misha, I have looked for her, to no avail. I asked her mother about her, but she hadn't heard from her either.

I've never stolen a car, but I did lose one of my mother's really nice rings when I was a teenager. I told her about it a few years ago and I asked her if there was any way I could replace it. Surprisingly, she didn't appear angry and she forgave me.

We all have something that we need to be forgiven for. I wish Misha the best.

His Promise

The heart is deceitful above all things, and desperately wicked: who can know it?

- Jeremiah 17:10

My Promise

I promise to continue to show up for loved ones that need me, even if there is a chance that my car may be stolen.

Less is More

As a public speaker, author and poet, I don't have a problem with self-disclosure. I don't believe in full disclosure while I'm teaching a workshop, but I can over share in my personal life sometimes. While at my internship, I spoke with one of the supervisors, Diana, who seemed friendly and inviting. She was always interested in what I was saying, and we hit it off. So I thought.

I mentioned to her that I was writing a book and she said that she proofreads and that she would love to read it. I told her I had an editor, but it couldn't hurt to get an opinion on one of the stories. When she started reading it, she noticed that it mentioned my daughter – a detail she didn't know about me. I went on to explain everything that happened, and why I didn't mention her before. A few people in the office knew about her, but we hadn't had the opportunity. I know I was long winded, but that is part of me that I am working on. I always have to prove that I am not lying. Even if no one is interested.

About twenty minutes into our conversation, I noticed

her texting someone. She kept speaking to me casually, but thirty seconds later, someone knocked on the door. It was her friend and co-worker, Brittany, and she had an emergency for Diana to take care of. I knew this was a brush-off. I told her that I will see her later and I left her office.

That night, I tried not to obsess over this situation. I had to accept that I need to work on my approach when I meet someone new. I don't have to explain myself, or overly correct something that is going on in my head. She would have been fine with, "Yeah, I have a daughter." When she asked her age and where she was now, I could have answered that and stopped there without the need to validate her absence. My advice to myself when meeting someone new, is KISS (Keep It Simple Stupid).

I told myself that my workplace is my work place and I decided to treat it that way. Since I am so sensitive about things, I had to purposefully keep a good attitude. I made sure to continue to greet everyone, but I did not engage in conversation unless someone else initiated it. Even then, I offered the appropriate amount of feedback, and I was genuinely interested, so I was not being rude.

On my way to the bathroom one day, Brenda said, "You're being awfully quiet today."

I simply replied, "I talk too much, but I'm working on it."

When I came back to the front, another co-worker, Karen, was talking to the supervisor, Diana. She stopped mid-conversation and turned towards me. Turning back to the supervisor, she said, "She smiles too much for me. Just too much."

I can't please everybody. This is an example of being too full and trying too hard. I struggled with this well into my thirties. My daughter and I go through stretches where we don't speak for periods of time and at that time, I was caught off guard and feeling ashamed and guilty. I tried to receive validation from a stranger who held no weight in my life, and I ended up dumping on her. In psychology, we would say that I had porous boundaries. I gave too much information to people who weren't invested in me. I struggled between having porous boundaries and having rigid ones. Rigid boundaries aren't any better, it stops people from really getting to know anything about me.

Now I have found a balance, it may not be perfect, but I share when I feel compelled to do so. It's okay to keep things private, in fact it's appropriate in some settings. Now I have an awesome support system that I can talk to, and receive all of the validation or correction that I can handle.

Work is for working. I have made a few lasting relationships with co-workers, but those relationships were formed outside of the workplace. It's important to remain professional in a professional setting.

His Promise

A man of knowledge uses words with restraint, and a man of understanding is even-tempered. Even a fool is thought wise if he keeps silent, and discerning if he holds his tongue.

-   Proverbs 17:27:28

My Promise

I promise to set healthy boundaries.

Spent in Sprint

In my early twenties, I was in what I thought was a committed relationship. I was 'shacking up' with a guy that I had been dating since I was a freshman in high school. This boyfriend and I went to a cell phone store one day. Instead of him checking out the phone, he was busy checking out the cute girl behind the counter. It was so blatant that she felt uncomfortable and tried to hide her face behind the luscious curls that hung past her earlobe.

I finally said something to him like, "Ummm, okay, we are looking at the phones, but do you want her number or something."

He replied, "I was trying to see if she had a face under all of that hair."

At that point she removed the hair from her face with her pointer finger and placed it behind her ear. She was fully flattered and I was fully pissed. I finished up my business and left the store, with my disrespectful boyfriend reluctantly following behind me. Halfway through the parking lot, he said he forgot something and ran back into the store. I didn't follow him or question him any more about it. I started making plans to remove him from my house and my life.

I recount this one experience because it shaped my dating life. It made me extra cautious whenever I went on a date with a guy. If he had a wandering eye, I made a mental note and wrote him all the way off. I did not have time to follow up behind some horny toad and work on my insecurity issues. I figured that the person I would really settle down with, would only have eyes for me. He would be sent from God and we would not be living in sin. Fornication is wrong, and while I committed myself to him, he was not sent to me by God.

Married or not, whenever someone cheats, I believe it is premeditated. Lust begins in the mind. It had to have been constructed in a thought before it was acted upon. When a man sleeps with a woman it's not happenstance. There is some planning that took place. When the opportunity presented itself, he made it happen. If sleeping with someone just happened, that same excuse could be used for anything, "Oh babe, I'm sorry. I didn't mean to sleep with your dog, it just happened." This scenario is less likely to happen because it's rarely something that men think about. Note that I said, rarely.

It took me years to get over this incident. I was insecure and I felt that everyone and anyone was better than me. I was already a wreck and this just played into my insecurities. I learned the hard way that we teach people how to treat us. I treated myself like I wasn't worthy of love and fidelity, so why should he? I was still figuring life out. We stayed together for much too long and ended up breaking up after he gave me a concussion, which I believe affects my spatial memory to this day.

Self-work is necessary at any age. I was aware of my issues, but help wasn't as available as it is now. My hope is that young women and young men love themselves first and allow that to be enough.

His Promise

The righteousness of the upright will deliver them, but the unfaithful will be caught by their lust.

- Proverbs 11:6

My Promise

I promise to believe that I am enough.

A Way of Escape

Growing up with the issues I had, I looked for love and affection in all the wrong places. There were times when I did things to hurt, for attention or simply to feel wanted. Additionally, I have had my moments. Times when weakness occurred because it was on my mind, even subconsciously; and eventually, 'it went down.' Then it's the agony of the next day, or the next date. There is no reversing the past, but there is redemption.

The questions that surfaced: "I wonder if he'll think I'm easy." "What does he think of me?" "Will I ever hear from him again?" The shame, the guilt, the stress to redeem your true-self, never seems to be enough. The praying and repenting helps your relationships with Jesus, but what about with him – the new guy that you slept with way too fast?

There is that awkward moment the next day; where you wonder whether or not you should call him and explain yourself. The passion overcame you, it's been a while, and you had no idea that was going to happen. Leave out the part about you shaving your legs, just in case. Finding out his last name, address and home telephone number should also be included in this conversation. Well, all have sinned and have fallen short of the glory of God. That's what we say when we talk about ourselves being unholy.

Some women have accidentally found themselves in this predicament several times. We live and we learn. When I was dating, I found a few tips to help me stay safe.

✔ Never invite a guy home until we have been on at least three dates and I have his address.

✔ Don't drink on the first date or at all, which was easy, because alcohol wasn't really my thing.

✔ Do something outdoors if the weather permits, like miniature golf.

✔ Drive my own vehicle and meet him there.

✔ Keeping my own morals and values at the forefront of my mind wasn't always easy, but necessary.

I started using my "dating tips" when I got sick and tired of getting played, getting used and playing house to someone who didn't deserve that much time and attention. Sometimes all I could do was stop and wait and allow God to move mountains. I had to ask for help though. God was present, but I found that He worked better when I called on Him. He made Himself known when I sought His face and guidance. There are situations that I know I could have called on Him and He would have been there, but my flesh wanted what it wanted and I gave in to what I wanted instead of what I needed. Each of those situations ended in some type of heartache or disappointment.

When we find ourselves in situations that are uncomfortable and we feel pressured to go all the way, there is a way out, and it could be as easy as saying "no." At times I had moments of regret and I felt like being "good" was too hard. I would call my dad and complain about these rules and restrictions being placed on regular people like me. I would say that it just wasn't fair and God knows that it's so tempting out here. My dad would say the same verse every time I argued this point with him.

His Promise

No temptation has seized you except what is common to man. And God is faithful; he will not let you be tempted beyond what you can bear. But when you are tempted, he will also provide a way out so that you can stand up under it.

-    1 Corinthians 10:13

My Promise

I promise to utilize "a way out" when needed.

The Wrong Medicine for Heartbreak

Some people say that the best way to get over someone is to get under someone else; that is the worst advice ever. Feelings are bound to get hurt and no one wins. Being a rebound is a hard job, and no one should have to do it.

In my early twenties, I ended up breaking someone's heart, because I was not over an ex, and I wanted to move on. The new guy was adorable; caramel complexion, green eyes and a little swag. I liked him, but we should have taken things much slower. By the fourth month, I was taking care of him like a nurse, because he had cancer. I had no idea and it wouldn't have been a deal breaker; but it was a lot to deal with. I wanted to help him, heal him, fix him and I could not turn my back on him during this time. I liked his family, and they liked me, until I broke his heart.

I got with him after I found out that my ex had been cheating on me. The heartbreak was still fresh, so I was still semi-stalking my ex. We didn't have social media, but I called my friends who knew what he was up to and got the scoop through them. So when he tried to win me back, I didn't make it impossible for him. I actually went to his house and spent the night.

While there, I ignored the dozens of phone calls from my boyfriend; I wanted to get back at my ex for hurting me. The plan was to give him the night of his life and make him miss me and then leave forever. Looking back, I was an idiot. I admit that. Growing pangs are free and plenty. Of course that plan backfired, because my expectations were way higher than what that night ended up being.

The girl that he cheated on me with came by. He professed his love for me, while I stood in the living room in a towel, disappointed. Only for me to tell the girl that she could have him. She went on to say that she knew he loved me, and all he did was talk about me. I thought I would celebrate this moment, but I felt horrible. I had someone at home who really cared for me.

When I went home the next day, he had been up all night, vomiting, sick to his stomach with worry. He had been in remission, but I can't help but wonder if I added to his later fate. Our downstairs neighbours, who happened to be my landlords, had been up consoling him. When I saw them, I came up with some lame excuse. The pain in those beautiful emerald eyes pierced my soul and all I could do was beg for forgiveness. I finally admitted my true motives and feelings.

The next day when I came home from work, he had moved out, with the new refrigerator that he bought me. I felt a sense of relief and a heavy guilt at the same time. I was a mess. It was inevitable that I would see him again since we worked together and after another sincere apology, we became friends. After a few years we lost contact with each other. Later, he lost his fight with cancer. I am so glad that we made amends, and that I didn't leave him with that horrible image of myself. I am glad he had the heart to forgive me, a foolish, love sick, stupid girl, that didn't know which way was up.

The issue was that I had no business dating anyone. I understand now that every soul I had sex with became one with me. It took several years to heal from these encounters. Although I can count my sexual partners on one and a half hands, I still felt the emotional effects of each of them. As a woman I am a receiver of their spirit. So they deposited their issues, fears, insecurities, anger, unresolved mommy and daddy issues into me every time we were intimate. That's a lot of baggage added to my own. No wonder I was a mess. I was hurt and I hurt others.

I was not cut out for the dating world. There were too many moving variables. I'm sure it would have been different if I had been healed and whole, but I wasn't and I left damage in my wake. I wanted revenge and ended up hurting an innocent person. Thank God he forgave me before he passed away. It took years to forgive myself.

The ex that I cheated with, and later left, married the girl that came over that night. They ended up getting divorced, after he cheated on her. I wish him and his ex-wife the best in life.

His Promise

Peace I leave with you, my peace I give unto you: not as the world giveth, give I unto you. Let not your heart be troubled, neither let it be afraid.

-   John 14:27

My Promise

I promise to return all past intimate relationships and spirits to their owners.

CHAPTER 4
Without Permission

Pseudo Control

One commonality that I have found while working with victims of sexual abuse is that they are usually victimized more than once, for various reasons. This is true in my case as well. During a time of my two-months bout with homelessness, I found myself working full time, but still sleeping in my car with my six-year old daughter. I moved from Madison, back to Milwaukee, to live with my mother who said she wanted to mend fences and work on our relationship. I was engaged to be married to a wonderful man, who had never done anything to deserve my abandonment. At that time, my relationship with my mother took precedence over anything else and I wanted to make it work.

I packed up and moved in with my mother, leaving my ex and his family devastated. I took my savings of about two thousand dollars with me. My mother was aware of my small savings and before the end of the first week, my money went to her various bills, all of which were emergencies, or so she said, or other desires she had.

By the second week, I was told that I was cock blocking and that I needed to move out. I pleaded with her to allow me to stay until I found somewhere else to live, but she wouldn't have it. I had to leave that day. I had not done anything to provoke her, the only problem was that I ran out of money. I felt the weight of the decision I made, and the thought of hurting my ex the way I did was unbearable. I tried to apologize, but he was very hurt. There was nothing I could do to console him. He came to visit me a few times, and I visited him, but things were never the same.

I was still working full time, but I didn't have enough money for a deposit on an apartment. My mother owned the duplex she lived in, where my brother lived upstairs, rent free, well, that's another story.

I'd been on my own since I was eighteen, and I had never been homeless. It was an adventure for my daughter; it was a nightmare for me. I thank God for friends who allowed us to come and bathe or sleep over. I didn't disclose my situation to most people, not even my closest friends. I didn't want anyone to pity me, or tell me, "I told you so." They were aware of the tumultuous relationship that I had with my mother and they would have thought I was crazy for leaving a fiancé, a stable home and his loving family for this pipe dream.

Most of the time we slept in my car, a 2002 Hyundai Sonata. It wasn't big, but we made it work. I usually parked behind an apartment complex of a friend for the night. I wanted to be somewhere familiar, and I was. One particular time, a man knocked on my window and scared me awake. I no longer felt safe and I knew that I had to get somewhere fast.

I was right across from a friend of mine that I had known since the fifth grade. We had been in touch periodically, and his daughter played with mine whenever we were in town. Since moving back to Milwaukee from Madison, we had spoken and had gone on a few playdates with our girls. I called him and asked if we could come by. He agreed, and I made a pallet on the floor right next to my daughter.

About an hour later, after my daughter and I fell asleep, I felt someone watching me. I woke up to find him standing at the foot of the pallet. At this time, I didn't know what was going on. I thought maybe he wanted to tell me something, but he came and laid next to me. He didn't say a word and I wanted to move, but I didn't want to put my daughter in harm's way.

I told him to quit playing, although I knew in my gut that this was far from a joke. He had flirted with me before, but he always respected my boundaries. I was afraid. I didn't want to wake my daughter up, and as he forcefully pulled my pyjama pants down, I tried fighting him off while holding my breath so that I would not make a sound. I had limited mobility, and my little girl was literally an arms-length away. He raped me. I couldn't believe it. A single father that I had known since the fifth grade raped me next to my daughter who happened to be the same age as his.

I was ashamed of being in this position once again. I was no longer the silly teen, but I repeated silly teen behaviours. I kept thinking about my daughter and how afraid she would be if she woke up while this man was assaulting me. When it was over, he walked back to his room, closed the door and I sat there next to my daughter until the sun came up.

Early the next morning, I rushed her out of the house to my female friend's house across the street where we took showers and ate breakfast. Once again, I went on about my day as if nothing happened.

While it may not seem like I was under the protection of God, I know that it could have been so much worse. I couldn't blame anyone for my situation, but me. I was an adult, making rash decisions that affected myself and my daughter. Although the pain of being violated made my heart heavy, I thanked God for allowing me to walk out of there alive, without my daughter being the wiser.

For several years I refused to talk about this incident with anyone. This incident was the catapult that pushed me into Mitch's arms. He had been trying to date me for several months and I had been avoiding him. One day he called and I told him that I had moved out of my mom's house and I was in-between homes. He asked me to come stay with him, but I didn't want to do that. I wasn't over my ex-fiancé and I wanted to get my own place. I had been homeless for two months and I had almost saved enough for the first and last month's rent and the security deposit.

Getting raped while lying next to my beautiful daughter put a fear in me that I couldn't explain. I called Mitch from work the next day and he got an apartment for us to stay in. He was my knight in shining armour. Who knew he would later use his sword against me?

His Promise

The angel of the LORD encamps around those who fear Him, and rescues them.

- Psalms 34:7

My Promise

I promise to nurture the part of myself that feels shame and guilt from being a victim of rape.

He's Still Here

Fathers leave, mothers too, and so do children, husbands, and wives. Friends and family members will leave, and having pets and possessions permanently, is not guaranteed. We may have to deal with abandonment, divorce, affairs, careers, education, addictions, incarceration, selfishness, military duties, and death. Whatever the reason, loss and sudden change, being forced out of our comfort zones cause hurt and can leave a hole in the heart that seems to never get filled.

I've dealt with a lot of loss and changes in my life and I thought I would spend a lifetime trying to fill the void by making unhealthy life decisions. I've often expected someone else to live up to the ideal of the last one that left. I replaced my mother with my friends' moms. I replaced a loving fiancé with a bad husband. I replaced old friends with new ones. It was a never ending cycle, one that I had to learn in order to break free from.

When it comes to a romantic relationship, I've read that it takes about one third of the time invested in a relationship to heal from that relationship. Healing should also be done before getting into another romantic relationship. If a parent, friend or family member has left, grieving is still very natural and necessary for healing. Holding on to anger and putting up walls is a recipe for loneliness. It's necessary to accept the truth, grieve and continue to explore, love and meet new people, free of expectations of them replacing the one that got away.

My ex-husband promised to never leave me. Our marriage was a disaster and everyone watching waited for it to implode. I made a decision to change my life. I knew that I had to make a decision to heal or be broken for the rest of my life, so I decided to heal. He didn't like the new confident, God fearing me. He resented the fact that I had forgiven my abusers, continued my education and showed kindness to him in spite of his hatred towards me.

For a year, I prayed for God to fix our marriage, to help him and soften his heart. Finally, I prayed for God to fix our marriage or take it away from me. Three days later, he left. It hurt, but I knew that it was God. Sometimes the people we choose are not the ones God chose for us. We have to accept that reality, and allow them to leave without guilt or condemnation. I believe that someone that leaves me was never mine to begin with. If we accept that God knows best, it will be easier to deal with change.

I was twenty eight when Mitch and I moved to Alabama. I learned that I couldn't sprinkle poop with sugar and expect it to be sweet when I married Mitch against the will of God. I knew we weren't supposed to get married and I suffered dearly because of my disobedience. Not only was my life affected, but so was Mikey's. We have to be mindful in who we choose to procreate with. We can't expect a perfect childhood for our children, when we fail to choose the perfect mate. I don't expect true perfection, but a perfect mate for me. It took thirty one years to marry my soulmate, but I wasn't even allowed to meet up with him again until I was on my healing journey. I wouldn't have had to mourn a marriage and suffer through a divorce had I listened to God in the first place.

His Promise

He [God] Himself has said, I will not in any way fail you nor give you up nor leave you without support. [I will] not, [I will] not, [I will] not in any degree leave you helpless nor forsake nor let [you] down (relax My hold on you)! [Assuredly not!]

- Hebrews 13:5

My Promise

I promise to ask permission instead of forgiveness from this point forward.

Hurricane Mitch

Pain brought my ex and I together, by trauma bonding, but with my metamorphosis, we had grown apart. I was finding joy and peace and he was still imprisoned. I never pushed him, but I invited him to receive this gift that I had been given; I prayed for him and with him, but in the end it was his choice, and he chose otherwise. Thank God.

Mitch and I separated seven months after moving into our home, I was twenty eight at the time. There is something really low down about someone leaving me and lying on me to make themselves into the victim. He perfected this skill and I was devastated to learn that he had been building a case against me from the very beginning. I later learned that these are common traits of a narcissist. They create a false narrative against their partner, so when they need to make their escape, they look like the one that tried to make things work and they finally had to succumb to their need to protect themselves.

Mitch has been married four or five times and he is only forty-five years old. He has done this to every woman he has married or dated. I feel for every woman who has suffered the wrath of Hurricane Mitch who leaves destruction in the wake of his path. Unfortunately, there is no way to warn these women, as they will see you as the bitter ex, who wants their new lover back.

His ex-wife tried to warn me when I first became enthralled in his love bombing, and while I didn't disrespect her, I didn't take her seriously. He had already set her up as his ex who cheated on him, and left him for another man. He said that she regretted her decision and wanted to get back with him. This story made him seem even more valuable to me, I needed to secure my spot in his life before she was able to win him over.

When he walked away, he left a whirlwind of destruction behind him. In order to discredit me, he lied to our creditors, making me out to be a lying cheating wife who abandoned him and took away his son. In every scenario he was always the victim. I received a seven day notice to vacate our home, since he hadn't paid the mortgage in six months. We had only been there for seven months.

He had been renting the furniture and hadn't paid that in weeks, they repossessed that as well. My truck note had not been paid, in fact, he told them that I had left him for a man in Waukegan, Illinois, and that was three months behind. I had just paid the $348 utility bill myself. He had been planning his escape for months, and he wanted sympathy from total strangers. Later still, I found out that he had opened businesses in my name and used my name for several purchases that he may never pay.

God had been preparing me for this very moment. I had already begun my healing experience, and I was seeking a closer relationship with Him. I had gone through a biblical counselling plan and it really helped me to understand who I was and why I was so broken. Better yet, it helped me to heal and forgive. We were no longer a match. Although it took time for me to understand this, it was all God's doing.

I have learned not to let my emotions drive the car, they can give directions, but my mind will be the driver.

His Promise

See that no one repays anyone evil for evil, but always seek to do good to one another and to everyone.

- 1 Thessalonians 5:15

My Promise

I promise not to make long lasting decisions on temporary emotions.

Pain is Pain

Being cheated on hurt me in places that I didn't know existed. Discovering the truth about my ex-husband's affairs was devastating. The truth is that it was a blow to my ego. I wondered what I did wrong and what she was doing right. For some women, it can become a competition between the wife and the mistress and the only one who wins this battle is the husband. I knew that the cheater was the one who must decide whether to seek comfort outside of the marriage or to seek to repair the marriage. Married couples are not the only ones that suffer when the one they love cheats on them. I believe that teenagers, young adults and adults that allow themselves the freedom to love and trust all take a risk. When someone makes a commitment to be faithful and honest, and they break that commitment, it is very painful.

I never dismiss the power of relationships, and the level of commitment that come with them. It is important for married people to comfort their single friends who have suffered the heartbreak of a cheating partner. I remember suffering through heartbreak alone, because my married friends would say, "At least you weren't married, it would really hurt." Parents should take into account their own experience of being young and having their first loves as well. They should be more understanding of and open with their teens and allow them to be honest about their feelings.

When a spouse breaks the sanctity of a marriage by committing adultery, or when a loved one promises to be faithful and if they break that promise, it's up to the one that is hurt to forgive them and leave or forgive them and stay. Either way, forgiveness is what will allow the one that is hurt to heal. God promises to be a huge part in the healing process.

His Promise

He heals the brokenhearted and binds up their wounds.

-    Psalms 147:3

My Promise

I promise to respect everyone's journey married or single.

CHAPTER 5

Restoration

What we Feed Grows

My biggest fear in life has always been being a bad mother, or being a good mother and my children still thinking that I was a bad mother. I've always gone above and beyond making sure they knew I loved and cherished them. It has not always gone the way that I planned, and so I've learned that, parenting out of guilt or fear is very damaging.

I have experienced this first hand and all I ever wanted for my children was to keep them safe. From the very first time my daughter met my step-daughter who had been in the system before my ex-husband got her, my daughter started making up stories about being in foster care as well. The girls were only one year apart, ten and eleven years old, and we did a lot of fun things together. One thing we did was start a book club, just the three of us. We would go to Barnes and Nobles and pick a book for the week. Well, one week the girls chose the book, "A Child Called It."

This was a teaching tool for me, since the girls were both abused at different stages of their lives. I wanted them to see, in addition to counselling, that they can be successful. One day, the girls were caught misbehaving; this was after we moved into a bigger home to give them their own space.

We told them that if they were caught doing this thing again that they would be punished. My ex-husband spanked his daughter and I spanked mine. That night, the girls corroborated a story full of lies to tell their teachers about us. His daughter did have a mark on her behind from the spanking, although I didn't know it at the time. They were so angry that they used all they had read in that book against us.

When I went to pick them up from school with my four month old son, they weren't outside. I never allowed them to catch a school bus. Once I walked into the school, I was interrogated, and my son was snatched from my arms. I didn't see any of them for five days; it was a holiday weekend and the offices were closed for a few days. My daughter really did get to see a foster home and my mother who never wanted to be bothered with me or my daughter became very much involved. She formed a coup with my daughter and our relationship has never been the same since.

My daughter ran away repeatedly and hated the fact that I had another child after her being the only child for ten years. Counselling was working well for the first year, but my mother's negative influence and my daughter's manipulation became toxic. The therapist requested that I sign over my rights altogether, but I wanted my child and I didn't want her to be away from me. The same system that failed my child years before was condemning me based on statements from my mother who didn't even know me.

I fought for my daughter in court for two years. I was accused of every lie a person can tell. Every claim was a lie and found unsubstantiated. Finally, I agreed to allow my mother visitation, a sort of temporary custody, during the summer. I visited regularly.

On one of my visits, I noticed my mother and brother packing boxes. When I asked her about this, she said she was spring cleaning. My mother had been in this home for over twenty-five years and it was cluttered. I called my daughter and dealt with my mother's accusations and verbal abuse daily. I visited every few days, and the last day

I showed up, the house was empty. My mother kidnapped my daughter.

It would be months before I found them. When I did find them, I bought tickets to visit them in Pennsylvania. My mother refused to let me see my daughter or talk to her. I was devastated and it didn't occur to me that this was another way that she could abuse and control me until very recently. I had never been so hurt, or felt so betrayed as I did at that moment.

The best thing that has ever happened to me are my children. My mother knows that, she has always known that. It was even more hurtful that my brother and some family members that I never spoke to helped her. No one reached out to me, no one double checked her stories, considering our past.

I begged for my daughter to come back home and I warned her that a lack of rules, which included a lack of counselling, did not mean more love. She refused to come back to me for years. After two years of living with my mom, she too had succumbed to the physical abuse that I experienced for as long as I could remember. Finally, the state removed AJ from my mother's care for excessive physical bodily harm, including choking her, and trying to push her over a balcony. Those accusations were substantiated.

It took years, but I forgave my mother. In the process of forgiving her, I learned that I had to forgive myself, my family and my daughter for the part that they played in this. It's still a struggle to overcome the shame, guilt and betrayal. I am not perfect, but I love my children and I always do what's best for them. It took a while for my name to be cleared of wrongdoing, but God restores in His time.

This experience taught me a valuable lesson. One of my greatest fears was that I never wanted to be separated from my children in any capacity, but the more I focused on that, the further AJ ended up away from me. I learned first-hand that what we feed grows. I fought for my daughter who wanted nothing more than to be with the very woman who ended up breaking the toilet with her head. AJ disclosed these experiences after she left my mother's home.

I would like to say that I didn't know why she wanted to be there but I can't. AJ's relationship with my mother is no different than mine was. I loved her dearly and I chose her over my nurturing father more than once. He was very religious and I could hardly get away with anything with him. With my mom I had a little bit more freedom and all I had to deal with was 'a little abuse here and there.' I guess in wanting what was best for my children, I caused AJ to want to be in a more lenient home environment.

His Promise

But all things become visible when they are exposed by the light, for everything that becomes visible is light.

-   Ephesians 5:13

My Promise

I promise to forgive myself, my mother and my daughter, and to accept where we are at this very moment.

Protecting my Peace

At age 28, I was able to name the level of hypersensitivity I was born with. I learned that I am an empath. I cannot change that fact about myself, but I can change how I respond to things. It's difficult feeling the needs of others in the pits of my belly or having images of abused children and animals, or battered women, and men who succumb to police violence or any violence. It's a harsh world that we live in. I have literally prayed for God to remove the part of me that feels this deeply.

There are too many things that can disrupt my peace. The news is one of them. Now I avoid it at all costs. If God had not gifted me with empathy and compassion, I would have avoided being an advocate and social worker. I have never been able to let things go easily, which is why I hate the news. The media contorts stories to invoke fear, prejudice or disbelief and there is hardly anything worth watching, besides the weather.

Every animal commercial with the shivering puppy, or the dog with the patches of hair missing and the one that is stuck in the cage looking so pitiful, makes me want to drive to a shelter and get every cat, bird and dog there. The commercials of hungry children are what lead me to sponsor children in Africa with money that I did not have. Then there are the St. Jude's commercials that make me cry, while I sit in the middle of my floor writing checks that I cannot afford. There is also the sexual abuse prevention movement that I am deeply involved with. Each of these causes are wonderful, but I am one person, and quite frankly, I have to choose where I spread my energy.

I understand why my clients used drugs to numb their pain. That isn't an option for me, but I did use food as a way to cope. In my quest for healing, I have to unplug. Things affect me deeply and the effects are lasting, so I have to be diligent in what I choose to consume. I cannot stop every painful thought, and I cannot mute my clients from telling me of their trauma. I am very present and aware when I am providing therapeutic services for my clients, but I have learned to allow them to own their own pain, progress and accomplishments. I will sit with them, listen to them and sometimes cry with them, but their experiences are their own. It has taken several years for me to get to this place and I still have growing to do in some areas, but it has made my life so much better.

It is not my job to fix everything, I can't. I am not God. I have to allow God to do His job and fall back. I need to support others who support what they were created to do. At the same time I need to change my focus. I find myself exhausted at the end of the day, from enthralling myself into the lives of others. There is so much wrong in this world that it can become all consuming. There is also so much to be thankful for.

I know myself well enough to know that I tend to take on causes and internalize other's pain. I haven't perfected leaving it at the door, and since I know my limitations, I decided to remove all negativity from my life. This includes but is not limited to: family members, friends, certain television shows, social media and music that creates negative emotions within me. Since making this decision (in addition to taking my meds regularly), I have found myself much happier. It's been easier to get through the day, because I am walking in my purpose. I am so glad that

I am not God, I couldn't imagine that weight on my shoulders. I am content being one woman, with one cause and one God who can do anything.

His Promise

He is before all things, and in Him all things hold together.

-   Colossians 1:17

My Promise

I promise to allow God to do His job and to only own my experiences and the outcomes from them.

God's Got It

Restoration of my faith in God came only when I decided to depend on Him fully. As a child, I loved Him completely. I didn't want to disappoint Jesus, something that my father used to tell me. Now I know that he said this often to help me understand the weightiness of my actions as well as, as a tactic to keep me in my place. As I grew up, I began experiencing different things. I felt the pain of abuse and abandonment. I became a different person. I left God, but He never left me.

It took some time, but I was forced to my knees and it was the best thing that ever happened to me. Before I prayed for God to intervene in my life, I had become trapped in my mess. I wasn't happy, but I didn't want to give up my lifestyle. I didn't struggle with addiction to drugs and alcohol, but I sabotaged everything that was good in my life. I had a great job doing what I loved, and I owned my own business. I was addicted to pain and chaos. I had everything that I could ever want, except love, peace, and salvation. Looking back now, I didn't really have anything and everything that I had, meant absolutely nothing.

In the beginning of my newly found love for God, He answered every prayer that I prayed, no matter how trivial. He knew that I needed reassurance that He could hear me. I was still a babe, and as a babe, I needed a sign. The goodness in God allows Him to know me inside and out; He knows what we need and He loved me enough to give it to me. My faith grew and my prayers changed. I didn't need signs, I just trusted that everything would be okay.

Before I remarried, I was between checks and on the verge of getting evicted, and at the last moment, on the last day of the notice, God sent my friend by with the exact amount that I needed. She had no idea what I was going through. He's sent a couple by with groceries when I had run out of food, and I only fed my son, and ate what he didn't want. I never went hungry, but didn't have a lot. God has a habit of showing up in the eleventh hour, and I've learned that if I just keep the faith and wait on Him, or keep the faith and move when He says, "Move," everything will be alright.

Being without sometimes reminds me of the liberty that I have to call on God to supply all of my needs. God needs us to be humble in order to move the way He wants to in our life. That doesn't mean that I don't stress sometimes, I am human, but I try not to stay in that state of mind for long.

I remember having this experience when Mickey was a three-year-old. He was always so observant. He noticed that I was anxious about repaying a debt, and a check that I was waiting for was late. I made myself physically ill with worry. He came to me and said, "Mommy, we should just pray about your check, don't worry." He prayed with me and instantly I was reminded that God is not a trinket that I admire sometimes. He is tangible and very real.

I was 29 years old and I remember this day like it was yesterday. I was in undergrad and I was living off of my student loans. Oakwood University decided not to distribute the student loans on time. I later learned that colleges do this to earn the interest on the loans, I'm not sure if this is true, but someone who worked in the financial aid office told me. At the time it didn't matter why, I just knew that it really caused a lot of issues.

I was a master at budgeting at this point, but I couldn't

always make ends meet. God provided for me utilizing my friends, Jacine, Kim and Tim and he brought them to me sometimes in the eleventh hour. Many people showed up and showed out for us. I never had to ask for help, nor would I let them know what I was going through. AJ was with my mother in Connecticut at this time and I only had Mikey. I still think about these moments and remain humbled and grateful for God's grace and loving mercy.

His Promise

Therefore do not be anxious, saying, 'What shall we eat?' or 'What shall we drink?' or 'What shall we wear?' For the Gentiles seek after all these things, and your heavenly Father knows that you need them all.

- Matthew 6:31-32

My Promise

I promise to be obedient and allow God to use me to help others, the way He used others to help me.

Remarriage

Once my ex-husband left, I did some serious soul searching. For two years, I worked on myself and my son. I worked on rebuilding a relationship with my daughter and I wanted to know my mother better. I wanted to become all that God had created me to be. I wanted to be free. I didn't date, I did talk on the phone to one guy briefly, but when that became inappropriate, I cut all ties and changed my number. I always tried to keep my ex abreast of what was going on with our son, but he wasn't receptive. He tried coming back a time or two, but he hadn't changed and I wanted nothing to do with him, other than allowing him to be a father, something he rejected.

It took me thirty-one years to finally meet the man that God had for me. A childhood friend from Wisconsin, but I met up with him here in Alabama. What are the odds that we would meet here, miles from our hometown in Wisconsin? He had his own victory of freedom and he knew what it was like to be broken and rebuilt. We met, we prayed, we waited on God and we got married. Who knew that I would meet the man that I prayed for, with perks that I didn't know I wanted or needed?

There is no comparison between my ex and my husband now, but I can compare who I was with who I am. It has made the difference in my life. When I was broken I attracted pain, when I walked in faith and healing, I attracted a man of God. That's the difference.

I won't say that we are perfect, but we are perfect for each other. I give this praise to God. He was healing my husband, getting him ready, breaking addiction, removing strongholds, showing him love and how to love before he introduced us again. Had it been any sooner, I wouldn't have been ready and I would have ruined him with my mess. I must admit, in the beginning I was insecure and I didn't know how to trust, but he was patient with me. He was kind to me and he earned my trust and wiped away my insecurities, not with words, but with his love.

His Promise

She said to him, "Give me a blessing. Since you have given me the land of the Negeb, give me also springs of water." And he gave her the upper springs and the lower springs.

- Joshua 15:19

My Promise

I promise to trust God enough, to allow Quan to lead our family in the way that we should go.

Breath of Life

Having a child with physical and mental disabilities is very challenging to say the least. That's the nice way of putting it. Honestly, some days it is the most frustrating thing I have ever experienced. If Mikey only had a physical impairment that the world could see, it would be easier to remember that he is different. It may also help when I find myself explaining why I parent the way I do. Like, why I may seem overly protective, by not allowing him outside for an extended period of time without a responsible adult. Everyone has an opinion, and until very recently, I thought I had to at least consider them, but I don't and it is okay.

Mikey's health issues began at birth when the nurse held him in my birth canal until the doctor came to finish the delivery. This caused serious respiratory issues and on several occasions he choked on mucus. For the first 18 months of his life, he slept on either my chest or his dad's, out of necessity. After that, it was out of habit. Doctors acted as though they were at a loss and offered little to no help. Emergency room visits were the norm for us and I never thought he would live a full and healthy life.

Mikey was diagnosed with asthma and allergies and he has been hospitalized for both on more than one occasion. The food allergies were a little bit easier to manage. I could control what he ate, but the asthma was so severe that a flare up would occur at any moment due to the weather, a cold, or pollen. For the first year of my marriage to Quan, either he or I woke up every night to give Mikey his breathing treatments, honestly, it was mostly Quan. For the first five years before that, it was my job and mine alone.

Doctor appointments only lead to more medications and since the divorce from my ex, he was no longer around cigarette smoke which was a trigger. Triggers that caused these flare ups were scary. Finally, the best and the worst thing that could happen, happened. Two years into my relationship with Quan, Mikey's asthma had begun to flare up (age 6); I later found out there was mould in our apartment. Quan was literally a life saver for Mikey. He woke up nightly to provide Mikey with breathing treatments when he would wake up coughing due to a lack of air, that was his sign that he was having an asthma attack.

This one particular day, Mikey ended up in Intensive Care Unit not because of mould, but because he made the decision to climb to the highest cabinet and eat a tablespoon full of peanut butter. He was deathly allergic to it, but by this time his mental health issues combined with his behavioural issues had caused these types of incidents to occur. This was the first time he went for the peanut butter I had hidden in the back of the highest cabinet. This was the beginning of a chain of events that would change our lives forever with Mikey. His desire to cause harm would soon include causing harm to Jack, our youngest son, myself and later Quan.

He was on a CPAP breathing machine for three days and he could not breathe on his own. The allergy had triggered his asthma and it did not look good for him, so, I was praying harder for him than ever. Thank God for answered prayers, because we met a great pulmonologist. He made us a promise on the first day that we met. He said, "I promise you, even though your son is unable to breathe on his own now, he will be able to run outside and catch a cold without going into crisis."

Mikey remained healthy and was not hospitalized for asthma for over three years. Sometimes God uses medication to help us and that is okay. My prayers were answered, my son was able to breathe without impairment or pain. I am willing to accept His help in whatever form He sends it.

His Promise

The Spirit of God has made me; the breath of the Almighty gives me life.

\- Job 33:4

My Promise

I promise to accept and thoroughly research medical and mental health assistance and be diligent in making sure my family receives the care that they need.

CHAPTER 6

Friendships:

Reason, Season and Lifetime

I found myself in a frenzy with my friends while in my mid-thirties. This time was pivotal for relationships for me, some of my friends had been a staple in my life and I loved and cared for them all for different reasons. I later learned that some friendships were toxic and I wasn't always the victim in the situation. I was a horrible roommate to Stephanie, and I take the "L" there. Once I learned more about setting healthy boundaries, I gained the wisdom needed to identify healthy and unhealthy traits in relationships.

I've had friends that I will consider friends for a lifetime. I've had friends come and go. I've been loved and betrayed by friends. I've been hurt and comforted by some. I've had some friends that I would call during a crisis, and others that were good for a laugh. I've been a good friend, and a not so good friend. I've been overly involved and not involved enough.

It takes time to learn how to balance life, love and friendships. This is a skill that I have yet to master. After my dad died, I took a personal inventory of people that I consider friends. The people who came to mind have been there for me and I've been there for them. Through the years, we have laughed, cried and shared. It has taken time, experience, prayer and my husband, to help me learn the difference between takers, fakers and friends.

One of my closest friendships is less than five years old, but I feel like I've known Toya my whole life. I have another friend, Jacine, and I've known her family for over thirty years and others that I've known for over fifteen years, like my sister Nubi. I have friends that are couples, like Kim and Tim, or friends who were once coupled up, like Corey and his ex that we do not speak of. I know I'm leaving someone out, but I'm not listing every friend, just the different types of friendships. Every single friendship that I have ever had has impacted my life in one way or another.

Sometimes I can meet someone, hit it off well, and never see them again. With others, I may meet them, get past the initial greeting, we may hang out once or twice and the relationship never evolves into anything. Sometimes they call and I make a mental note to call them back, but I never do. Cases of phone tag, a funny feeling about the person, or just a lack of time can stop a new friendship from budding in its tracks. The older I get, the smaller my circle of friends became. It took years before I recognized that some relationships were temporary, and once it has run its course, it's time to let it go.

Social media makes it easier to keep up with milestones in people's lives, but it's made me more distant as a friend. If I can click on your page and see what's going on in your life, I'm less likely to contact you via the telephone. I will like a picture, wish you happy birthday, and you may get an occasional inbox, but that's it. Actually, if we are not in touch via social media, chances are you haven't spoken to me much at all. This doesn't mean that I don't still care for people that I've known for years. I would love to talk to some of my girls that know more about me than I can remember. It just never seems to happen these days.

My experience with friendships has made me cautious, but not cautious enough. I am a genuine person, what you see is what you get. I am the same all of the time, with everyone. Since I have such an outgoing personality, I rarely think about someone not being genuine with me.

When I find out about a betrayal, or if I hear a rumour about myself, I am always surprised, but I shouldn't be. I hate to make the reference about myself as an unsuspecting puppy, but I can be like that sometimes. I love people, I love meeting people and hearing about people's lives and I love encouraging people. I have to learn to tame that zealousness and take things for what they are, not what I want them to be.

Friendships should be reciprocal. Each friend has something unique they bring to the table. No one friend should always be the giver, and no one friend should always be the receiver. Now I take inventory of the people in my life and I identify what I bring to them and what they bring to me. I also have to determine what I take from them and what they take from me, this includes emotional support, which can be more daunting than financial expenses.

Time is also valuable, and I have learned that I am an ambivert. I enjoy people, but I need my personal time to regroup or I'm no good.

I hope that when my friends, present or past, hear my name, they smile; and if I have ever hurt someone, my prayer is that I have the opportunity to ask for forgiveness and right my wrong.

His Promise

A righteous man is cautious in friendship, but the way of the wicked leads him astray.

- Proverbs 12:26

My Promise

I promise to be the type friend for others that I expect for myself.

Idealess

I met Natalie during a workout at my apartment complex. She seemed nice enough and she started up a conversation with me. Being the social butterfly that I am, I am often ready to converse. We talked and worked out. It turned out that she wanted to learn how to do workshops. She was interested in cleaning up debt and felt that our community does not talk about finances enough. I was excited.

I invited her to my house and offered to show her a basic workshop that I had just done for Alabama A&M University, for undergrads. My workshop, *Living in Your Purpose, Be Your Very Best,* was totally unrelated to hers, so there wouldn't be any conflict of interest... right? Wrong. I gave her a basic print out after showing her how I developed my workshops and she left.

The next time I spoke with her, she informed me that her true calling was doing workshops on purpose, and she went on to tell me that her life coach and her agreed that clearing one's debt and living in one's purpose are correlated. I absolutely agree with that concept, and I know that having debt can prevent you from living in your purpose and being your very best. I also know that my workshop idea helped her to figure that out. I instantly regretted giving her that print out and I could have just kicked myself. This was not the first time something like this had happened to me.

I kept my distance from Natalie but, since she lived in my apartment complex, we did see each other every so often. One day she popped by unannounced after my dad died. This was one of the few times my in-laws decided to visit and Natalie and I weren't really on a "drop by" basis. It would not have been as awkward, except my husband opened the door and there she stood, in very short shorts, posing like she was going on a blind date. She did not say a word and my husband stood there waiting for her to say something.

When I saw who it was, I introduced her and ushered her outside so that Quan could continue his visit with his parents in peace. In some ways, this interruption was a welcomed one. Things could get pretty intense with my mother-in-law. Natalie and I sat outside for about an hour and I walked her home.

We went inside and her husband was surprised to see that she had her hair freshly done. I thought it was odd that she parked her car in front of her apartment and came to my house unannounced, before checking in with her own husband, but I let it go. We talked for a few more minutes and she tried to convince me to come with her to the mall, but I was not appropriately dressed to be outside of my house. I would have never gone anywhere looking like that. I kept explaining to her that I was getting myself ready for the week and that I had on cleaning clothes, but she persisted. I finally convinced her that I was by no means going with her that day and I went home.

I tried not to read too much into it, but I had a bad feeling in my gut, and I have learned to trust my gut. I talked about my feelings with my girl, Toya, and she thought something was shady about it, since she does have my number and she did not call first and how she was dressed. I know that when I visit a friend I make sure my bits and pieces are covered and tucked in. Now, I would not dress provocatively around anyone but my husband. When I was younger, and single, I dressed like a single chick, but I would dress appropriately when I visited my friends who were in relationships and as a courtesy, I would call first. Quan later told me that she stood at the door sizing him up and that she looked flirty. He went on to ban her from the house like he did Tammy. My friend list was getting shorter by the minute.

I really didn't know what was up with Natalie, but I would rather cut my losses and move on before I found out the hard way. I could have walked away after the workshop fiasco, and I did in a way, but I wanted to give her the benefit of the doubt. When she came by, her intentions may have been to check on me, she could have been surprised to see my fine husband and she could have become speechless. I don't know her life, but I know that I have been through enough mess with females and males alike, to let anything slide when my instincts tell me otherwise.

I enjoy seeing people succeed, which is a good thing within itself, but it becomes problematic when I fail to set healthy boundaries, which is what happened a lot during my twenties to my mid-thirties. I've learned now that I can give someone the whole blueprint to my programs, but they can't deliver it like I can. When the issue becomes more personal than professional and I feel that the person is not safe, I listen to that.

As far as business goes, no matter what someone does with the information I share with them, or the information they take from me, I'm protected. My dreams, my passion and my wisdom can only be translated through my delivery. I don't mind sharing what I can now. I developed programs for victims and families of sexual abuse and trauma over twenty years ago, when there were no programs available after AJ was molested in day-care. I searched, and there was nothing; God gave me that. He gave every workshop, presentation, training and seminar thereafter as well. No one can take from me what God has for me, that goes for my professional and personal life.

His Promise

There a woman met him, with the attire of a harlot, and a crafty heart... With her enticing speech she caused him to yield, with her flattering lips she seduced him.

- Proverbs 7:10,21

My Promise

I promise to walk in my purpose and not in fear.

Promises Broken, Friendship Strained

People usually can't kick me in the gut unless I'm already down; this story is an example of that. I was in my mid-thirties when I began graduate school and I needed a babysitter for the boys during my internship. Quan had started a new job, and his schedule wasn't flexible enough for him to take off and change his hours. So I needed to reach out beyond my comfort zone and I am not sure why I thought my mother would be a good fit, but I was desperate. I had already purchased cameras for my home and I would have had access to watch anything that could have happened, but it still wasn't the best decision, looking back at it. I wish I had saved my money and prayed about it.

I needed a babysitter for my first internship, there was no getting around it. I had to be "in the field" for forty hours a week for eight weeks. I also took three classes on the weekend, but Quan worked second shift, so a sitter would be needed for about fifteen hours a week.

My mother and I were getting along better, and she and

my daughter had just visited. My mom had been to see me a few times, once for a month, another time for two months, we actually were getting along. We were all in a good place. I asked my mom if she would mind coming back here during my internship. My nannie cams were ready and I was comfortable enough for her to watch them at that time. I offered to pay her every week and pay for her round trip ticket. She did not agree right away, but the next time I spoke with her she did. She wanted some of the money up front and I sent at least one-hundred dollars.

During this time, I noticed she had become more distant. She had begun answering my calls less often and when we spoke she sounded rushed or irritated. I asked her if everything was okay, and she would tell me something to get me off the phone. Finally, my daughter told me that she had been telling her that I better pay her or she wasn't coming. My mother knows better than anyone that I always pay my debts and hers, so this was odd to me. I had a feeling that she didn't really want to do it, but she could have just told me.

When I called her to double check if she changed her

mind or not, she was short and irritated that I brought it up. I now had less than a week to find someone to keep the boys. I was a mess. If I missed this internship, I would have to wait a full year before I went back. If this had not worked out I would have been okay with that, because my kids' safety was much more important than my education on any given day.

After praying about it, an elderly friend of mine, Laura, called. We spoke often and visited each other almost every other week, if not more. We saw each other every week at church. I told her about my situation and she offered to keep the boys for free. I should have been relieved, because it seemed like a prayer answered, but I was always nervous leaving my little ones somewhere.

After speaking to Quan about it, we agreed that it would be fine. The boys loved Laura and her husband, Wille. I told her that I would not have her keep them for free, so I had to give her seventy-five dollars a week. I provided the boys' food and we dropped them off and picked them up. I wanted to make it as easy as possible for her. I appreciated her helping me out and I told her that every time I saw her.

I prepaid her for the first two weeks, and promised to pay her every two weeks after that.

I deposited my school money into Quan's bank account and because he owed a debt, they were able to actually take all of my money out of his account in addition to his pay check that was deposited the same day. I was devastated. This set us back in a major way. We did not have money for anything including pampers for another two weeks. Thank God for my Pastor, Reggie, who had pampers for us as well as other items. I explained what happened to Laura and showed her the bank statements. I promised her in writing that we would still pay her, but I wanted to let her know what was going on. I knew it would be at least two weeks before Quan got another check and I did not have any money available to me.

Laura did not mention it, but she was not happy. Her attitude changed towards us. I understood, but I reassured her that I would understand if she didn't want to keep them until we got this settled. She agreed to keep them, and we did everything we could to scrape up that money to pay her, including over-drafting our accounts. We did not miss our second payment.

For our third payment, I asked her if we could write her a check for more than the amount that we owed her, because by this time our bills were due, and our accounts were consistently over-drawn. I found out that banks usually have to cash a check to a third party. She agreed and without asking how much we were giving her, she took all of the money and left us without anything. Quan was pissed. I called her and explained that we owed rent, and utilities and we were going to pay her as well, but not the entire payment.

When I called her, I expected her to understand since I had been doing her hair for free and bringing her food. Instead she gave me a lecture, implying that I was using her. She said that the little bit of money that I was paying her wasn't that much and she was giving up her summer to help me out. I could not believe this. I apologized and made a decision to quit school right then and there. I was not perfect, but I was not a liar and I was not using her to keep my kids.

After many tears and hurt from the allegations, I drove

home. Later that night she called me and said that she would keep them, I didn't want her to at that point. When Quan came home, he and I discussed it. He was not having it, he said that I was half-way finished and she agreed to keep them. We were behind one week, but we needed to work that out. He spoke to her and we came to an agreement.

I offered to barter, and I created a website for her. My going rate for websites would have caught us up and she would have owed me in the end. I stayed up all night to work on her website. It was a task, but I only charged her two weeks payment for it, which was one-hundred and fifty dollars. We were finally caught up and I was able to pay her in full for the last four weeks without incident.

I was able to finish my internship, but I made a decision to extend my program so I would not have to take another internship for a year. This incident reinforced my caution when asking someone for help. I tend to get kicked the most when I'm down. I end up repaying debts ten times over, because I am so grateful to anyone who would help me. I even paid my Pastor back, and the items he gave us were donated to the church.

Laura and her husband, Willie, were good people and I appreciate the fact that they kept the boys, but the stress around Laura going back and forth with me was too much for me at that time. I was under a tremendous amount of stress and all I wanted was to provide my littles with a safe place to be for a few hours a week. I wasn't sure why that was so hard. I have learned that people in my life, even those who are closest to me, have a difficult time being there for me when I am in need. With the exception of my sister, Nubi, people tend to act out a little when I show vulnerability, and I understand that I have to take responsibility for that because I don't ask for help much. Even my dear husband, Quan, has had moments where he didn't quite know how to respond to my vulnerability, because I usually mask well.

Laura and I are still friends, but things are not the same. I did tell her how I felt about the situation and that it really hurt me. I reminded her that she offered to keep them for free, but I would not have asked that of anyone. I still thank her, and I appreciate her sacrifice, but I would not ask her to spit on me if I were on fire.

I did not ask her to keep the boys the second time around, in fact, God worked it out so that Quan's hours and mine don't overlap. Sometimes life happens and it reveals our true selves and our true friends.

His Promise

And we know that all things work together for good to them that love God, to them who are the called according to his purpose.

- Romans 8:28

My Promise

I promise to allow myself to be authentic in my vulnerability when I am with people I trust.

Crazy Chrissy

Chrissy was a neighbour of ours who shared an apartment with her husband and three children directly behind us. From the very beginning, my heart went out to Chrissy after she told me about the tragic death of her mother. At that time I had not lost a parent and could not imagine growing up without one of them. Despite her trauma filled past, she persevered. I admired her drive and ambition. She sung in a choir and owned her own cleaning business. She did what she could to make ends meet and I respected that about her. We ended up spending time together after our kids went to school and our friendship grew from there.

The more we spent time together, the more I realized there were some things that did not add up. She told me that her husband refused to buy food for the house and that she and her three boys were often hungry. I began purchasing pizza's for them whenever I ordered pizza for my family. Due to my pregnancy, pizzas were a staple for a while. If I bought food for me, I bought food for her. When I met her husband, Kenny, he was nothing like she described. In fact, I witnessed him giving her money on several occasions and she spent it on fast food instead of groceries. This was the cause for the "lack of food" some days.

Although I was very pregnant with Jackson, and on strict bedrest, I found myself running to Chrissy's apartment on a daily basis to prevent yet another tragedy. Quan and I were often called to referee fights and mediate arguments between Chrissy and her husband Kenny. We were often woken up by a knock on the door early in the morning, or by their arguments that we could clearly hear from across the walkway. Chrissy had a temper and would often pull out knives to threaten Kenny. Kenny would antagonize Chrissy and bring her to the point of violence often to prove a point, it was a toxic relationship. One incident almost cost Kenny his life; he has the scar across his chest to prove that. We referred them to our family therapist early on, but there was only so much she could do.

Most of the arguments were about Chrissy having affairs with random men. There were pictures in her phone and incriminating text messages. I tried my best to talk to her about this behaviour, but this was going on much longer than I had known her, so there wasn't much I could do about it. Quan talked to Kenny about his issues as well. The last straw for Kenny was when the police officer that Chrissy had an affair with responded to a call and accosted Kenny in his own house. We were called over on more than one occasion to act as witnesses and give statements to police officers. Being friends to a warring couple is a full time job.

Our families grew closer as we attended barbeques at their house and went out to eat together. At the last barbeque we attended at their house, I walked in on Chrissy being very flirtatious with a guy that she introduced as her brother and close friend. He was on the couch tickling her. Eventually, he pulled her on top of him and they continued on with this behaviour. After several minutes of watching this, I decided that it would be best that I go out and make sure Kenny did not walk in on Chrissy in his house. Kenny and Quan were at the grill and I wanted to keep it that way.

The more we spent time together, the less I opened up to Chrissy. I couldn't put my finger on it, but something wasn't right. We ended up spending more time with Kenny and talking him down from the latest episode. As time went on, the complications of my pregnancy made it impossible to do the simplest task without pain and contractions. Since Chrissy and I couldn't hang out as much outside of the house, she came by my home. Since I was aware of Chrissy's behaviour and her lack of concern for her marriage vows, I made it clear that she needed to call me before she came over. Very few people have permission to pop-up at my house and she was not one of them.

Of course, Chrissy tested my boundaries by coming by without permission and I reminded her that she needed to call first. Sometimes I let her in, other times I didn't. One day I went to the store and I told her that I would call her when I got back home. She waited until I left to come by to "bring me a drink." She knew Quan was here, because she often checked our patio door and if it was open, she could see us sitting on the couch. When she brought the drink to him, he called me. This seemed odd to me since I had just told her that I was leaving and she made it a point to pop-up when I was not home. When I came home, I confronted her about this. She denied any wrongdoing.

Over the course of the next few days Chrissy had gone on a warpath telling neighbours that I was insecure and that I was mad at her for bringing me a drink. She was pissed and that was okay. Within weeks she went all out on a smearing campaign telling her sister that I said things about her, and I had never met her. I only knew what Chrissy told me. I received threatening email messages from her sister posing as someone else. When I called her out, they stopped, but this had gone way too far for me.

My mother always says, "A hit dog will holler," and Chrissy was a hit dog. I must have said something that hit close to home for her because she went all out trying to assassinate my character. I have tried to prove away lies, talk down lies and debate with liars. My father always told me, "Hon, you can't talk down a lie, you have to live it down." I learned this the hard way with Chrissy. When I told Chrissy that I heard the lies she had been spreading about me, I decided then and there to cut her off completely. Eventually, she moved and Kenny filed for a divorce. I had hoped that they would work it out, but I understood them going their own way. Kenny remained our friend, but Chrissy didn't.

She did try to come by and explain why she lied on me. I told her that I forgive her, but that I could not be friends with her any longer. When I asked her to leave, she refused, and our argument put me in the hospital for three days with contractions. Jackson was born a week early. Years later, other neighbours told me things she said about me once I ended our friendship. It looks like I made the right call.

This was my first time setting healthy boundaries in the beginning of a new friendship and it didn't go very well. It had taken over thirty years to understand the value of being upfront and honest about expectations in the beginning. I believe I have gotten better with it now, but this was an extreme case of befriending a person with the characteristics of someone with borderline personality disorder. I had no idea how serious this was until she came by my home when I was pregnant with Jack and she wouldn't leave.

A part of my healing process includes listening to my instinct, that gut feeling that something isn't right. This is often ignored, by victims/survivors of abuse or neglect. The gut feeling has been muted so often that it no longer elicits a reaction. It took me years of learning how to trust myself again, before I noticed that gut feeling. Now when I have it, I say a prayer and I move accordingly.

His Promise

Whoever slanders his neighbor secretly I will destroy.
Whoever has a haughty look and an arrogant heart I will
not endure.

-   Psalms 101:5

My Promise

I promise to listen to my instincts, no matter how minor it
may seem.

I'm a Mother

I'd known Debra since I was five years old. Her mother, Cindy, and my dad were friends for years. They loved and fought like siblings. Debra was the friend I used to call when there was a crisis. I could never tell what she was thinking. She has a level head and is void of any outward emotion. She can see a twelve car pile-up, and not bat an eye, but she would be the one to organize efforts to assist the crash victims. She handles pressure very well.

She is a talented and creative wedding planner. She called me when she needed to vent, I would make her see things differently. I cheered her up and kept her laughing. I was the friend that kept the circle together; when there was drama I wanted to squash it and move on. We were there for each other.

Debra was there for major milestones in my life. She planned my first wedding. She organized my baby shower. She was there when my children were taken for five days. She didn't say a word, she sat on the couch and was just there for me. I will always appreciate these things about her.

With the good, there was bad. Taking responsibility for things was never her strong suit. She never felt the need to apologize for anything that she did. She didn't respect other people's property or space. She broke my radio and my friend's television. She's left cigarette holes in clothing and nail polish in my dad's carpet. Her son, Berry, poured chocolate ice-cream in the interior my friend's car. She's used DVDs as a plate to cut lemons on with a razor blade. She burned incense on the edge of my television without an incense holder, so the plastic melted on the television in the shape of an incense. I overlooked all of these things. I would confront her, and we would move on... I accepted that this is who she is. The same way she accepted me and my flaws that irritated her.

Unfortunately, sometimes our kids' behaviour can alienate us from our friends. Like mother like son. Berry failed to take responsibility for his actions and she supported him. He's done things before to my property, like putting a booger on a newly lacquered handmade skateboard Mitch made. Not only did Debra refuse to make him clean it off, she refused to make him apologize and thought it was absurd for me to suggest he did. She always felt that I was over the top, but I don't care who you are, that's just nasty. I just can't believe how she handled this situation between our boys.

One day, she needed a place to stay for a few days. I don't usually do houseguests, but I made an exception. My husband, Quan, and I opened up our two bedroom apartment to her and her family. I allowed her, her mother, and her growing teenage son, and their dog to stay with me for three days.

On the third day, while Debra was at work, her mother was getting their things together to leave. Berry, was in the room with my son. He was a thirteen-year old, two-hundred pound boy, that was taller than me. I told the boys to straighten up the room. I went to the store, and when I got back, Berry and Cindy were packed up and ready to go. Once Berry left, my son came out of the room holding his face. He looked terrified. It took a while for him to tell me, but finally he told me what happened.

He said that Berry had slapped him across the face and told him that he better not tell or he would really hurt him.

I was livid. He said that he told Berry's grandmother, Cindy, what happened, but she didn't do anything.

My first reaction was to run after the car, but they had already driven off. I called the grandmother and she corroborated my son's story. She said she wanted to let Debra handle it. I asked to speak to Berry and he said that he didn't do it at first. Eventually, he confessed. He said that he was annoyed, because Mikey kept asking him questions, and talking to him, so he slapped him. I told him that he had no right to put his hands on him, and he could have just told me or his grandmother. I told him that we could talk about it more later, but I wanted him to apologize to Mikey. He refused to apologize.

I called Debra who was at work during the incident and told her what happened. I know that this would surely be different from anything in the past, my son was in pain and terrified. I fully expected her to handle the situation better, but she agreed with her son. She did not make him apologize to my son. Yet, she fully expected our friendship to continue. We privately went back and forth on social media for a while, but came to no resolve. She felt that I was overreacting.

This was so confusing to me, because anyone who knows, knows how I feel about my children. I can deal with foolishness, but violence against my child is unacceptable. I am not holding her accountable for her son's actions, I am holding her accountable for not caring enough for my child to make him apologize. Her love for her son would not be lessened by holding him accountable. Her lack of concern for my child only further supported her son's violent act. They were not the same age, size or height. It was not a fight, a disagreement or a struggle, there is no way this was okay.

I stopped being her friend right then. I could never imagine inviting someone like that back into my life. My son was terrified of Berry and he still talks about it. He does miss Debra and Cindy, but they were all a part of this violent act as far as I am concerned. There was no getting around it.

It's been seven years since I've seen Debra, we recently reconnected on social media, after she requested to follow me. She was a great friend at the time, and I love her dearly, and when we stopped talking to one another I felt the loss of our friendship. I just can't understand why she didn't make Berry apologize for hitting Mikey. I watched her son grow up, and she watched mine. This was just really bizarre to me and my mind went to the fact that something else more serious could occur and she would turn a blind eye to that too.

After the trauma of my past with AJ being abused and her abusers receiving support from their family, to Mikey being abandoned by his dad and suffering from that, I couldn't let this slide. I wouldn't even let a bully at school slide after hurting one of my kids. I have been put out of the Christian school AJ attended after a bully in the sixth grade harassed my kindergartener for being "too black." I also hold my children accountable, it's not one-sided with me in my home. My children constantly hear about the consequences of their actions.

His Promise

The LORD trieth the righteous: but the wicked and him that loveth violence his soul hateth.

- Psalms 11:5

My Promise

I promise to be fair.

And Then There Was One

Debra, Tammy and I were once inseparable. If you saw one you knew the other two were somewhere close. Of the three of us, Tammy was the one who required the most of everything: time, patience and attention. I met her when I was twelve and she was sixteen. We both happened to get a ride from my friend's father and I gave her a wet-willy in the back of the car. I was too young to "hang out" so we weren't friends just yet. We saw each other in church, but we didn't hang out until I was in my early twenties.

I visited Tammy several times a week. She seemed like she could use a friend. She had two small girls when I met her; one was a new-born and the other was three-years old. The three year old loved her baby sister, and did everything for her. The new-born cried constantly, and I knew that Tammy could use a break as often as possible. Looking back now, I'm pretty sure Tammy suffered from postpartum depression. Usually I was able to calm the baby with a bottle and some cuddling.

I would come to Tammy's house and watch movies,

paint my toenails, and offer to paint hers. I would bring junk food and she would supply the occasional steak and onions, a specialty of hers. We didn't go out together much back then, no matter how many times I invited her. It took her a while to visit my house.

Many years later, she told me that she didn't like me for years, although I came by often. She said she would watch me from her window when I came by sometimes and all she could think of was, "Why is this girl smiling all of the time? Why is she always so happy and why is she coming to see me?" She said that she had never met anyone like me, and while I confused her, she wanted me to come over. She said she would rent or buy movies that she knew I would like, and watch me watch the movie. I guess that's how I got the nickname, "Eyeball," because she knew which movies would make me cry.

This vulnerability translated into my personal life. I would fight for what I believed in and if someone messed with one of my friends, they messed with me. As time went on, it seemed as though Tammy had one crisis after the next. One major one involved her ex-boyfriend who she accused of molesting her youngest daughter. Since I was self-employed as an advocate against child sexual abuse and neglect, this lit a fire under me and created a personal vendetta between me and her ex.

I used my knowledge, compassion and resources to help her get away from him. She used my knowledge, compassion and resources to add fuel to the fire that she knew I would extinguish, while she sat back and watched. There have been so many times that I put my own life on hold to assist her in the latest girl fight, or mediate misunderstandings between people who just did not understand her.

My ex-husband, Mitch, saw right through Tammy. He said that she was vying for my attention, and that she was trouble. He warned me about her, but I thought he was just being hateful. We had numerous arguments about our friendship. She needed me.

I was there for Tammy during every major milestone in her life. When she accused her ex, Ernest, of molesting her youngest daughter, I went all in. I couldn't understand why she did not receive the justice that she deserved. Being a mother of a daughter who was sexually abused, I understood her pain. I had no idea, she was just regurgitating what I'd been through and applying it to her own life.

Later, I would find out that it was all a lie. Not before I allowed her to tell her story on my website. I was served a cease and desist letter, and was threatened to be sued for libel. I was ready to fight this as well, when I approached Tammy, she totally abandoned me. I told her all I needed to do was post proof of his abusive behaviour and it would not be libel. She never addressed it again. I took it down and continued this fight along with many others.

I didn't question her story until I noticed how cordial they were around each other. My confrontations with Ernest usually came when Tammy was not around. I declared war on him and his family for supporting him. Tammy on the other hand, called him for rides to the grocery store and I found him hanging out at her house occasionally. I didn't understand it, but she always had a reason for his presence.

There were times she called me in the middle of the

night, because she was afraid to walk into her house alone. I would get out of bed, drive to her home and walk her and her kids inside of her home, past the drug attacks that stood outside of her door. The last time she called me for this, it was after midnight, and once again, I was asleep. I was pregnant and in my last trimester, and I still felt the need to help her.

Mitch was livid. He said I absolutely could not go, and he wasn't having it. I was upset until he said, "Shima, you are driving in the middle of the night to walk her inside, who's walking you back to your car? Who's watching your back and protecting you?" I thought about that. I called her and told her that I couldn't come. She was very upset, but I expressed the concern that Mitch had, and she simply said that she never thought about it like that.

I'd taken several trips to Minnesota, to support Tammy during her sister's untimely fight with cancer, that she eventually lost. Her sister, Gigi, and I had become friends, and by the time she passed away, she was like a sister to me as well. I couldn't imagine the pain Tammy must have been going through. Her relationship with her father was tumultuous and he said hurtful things to her and she expressed her pain to me. I wanted to help mend their relationship, so I asked for his number and we talked on the phone.

He accused Tammy of being selfish, narcissistic and everything but the child of God. I could hardly believe what I was hearing. I defended her at every turn. He was very unhappy with my response and he hasn't cared for me since. In fact, he refused to let me in the house the last time I drove to Minnesota to see Gigi. Tammy watched from the door, another fight that she allowed me to fight alone. I drove the six hours back home the next day with my teething son.

Several situations like this occurred between men and women alike. She never seemed to get along with anyone. There were women who felt that she was inappropriate with their man, asking them questions about porn when she was alone in the room with him. Even Debra and I went on brief hiatuses when Tammy became too demanding. I never told Debra what Tammy said about her, and I never told Tammy what Debra said about her either. I think we all had our own pet peeves and occasionally we needed to vent. I never wanted our relationship to end because of it.

When I left Milwaukee and moved to Alabama in 2007, Tammy, Debra and I kept in touch. Debra moved to Tennessee, so I visited her often. Tammy eventually moved to Alabama. She was able to get into a shelter in Birmingham for abused and battered women fleeing from their abusers. She was single at the time, but once again Ernest was accused of pursuing her in a high speed car chase across the highway. She filed a police report and that was her proof. She was good at this. I had no idea she would eventually move to my city, but when she showed up, I was happy to see her.

Since I did not have room in my two bedroom apartment, I called my friend Jacine's mother. I asked her if Tammy could live with them. I vouched for her, and she agreed. Ms. J did not charge her any rent, so Tammy had it made. It wasn't long before I had begun hearing about Tammy's inappropriate behaviour. She lacked boundaries with Ms. J and her husband. She knew the family almost as long as I did, but this was the first time she met Ms. J. She knew Jacine's dad and brothers. Both of her brothers were in the house from time to time. The flirting and inappropriate behaviour with them made members of the family uncomfortable. I tried to reassure them that she didn't mean any harm, but I ran out of excuses.

Tammy's youngest daughter was with her, but her oldest daughter was in Milwaukee with her dad. She wanted to get her back, so she called me and Quan to take her to an airport in Atlanta. I agreed without hesitation, of course. She was proud of her breast lift and she made sure she mentioned them every time she could. She bounced around and was very flirty. After five minutes of this, Quan walked inside of the house and later told me that he didn't trust her and neither should I. Finally, I realized, all of these people cannot be wrong. Her behaviour around my husband was so inappropriate that I had to talk to her about it. After our talk, she toned it down, but was still very much over the top around him.

Her daughter visiting was more important than my irritation and we picked her up. The visit did not go as planned and she eventually sent her back to her father in

Milwaukee, but some way she made it seem like he took her and would not give her back. I was well aware of what happened with Tammy, because I was there every day. This was a pattern with her.

Once she started spreading rumours about me, I knew it was time to cut ties. One thing I hate is when someone lies on me. I found out about the rumours when I visited Janice's good friend and neighbor, Sandra. We had so much in common. Our sons were the same age, they liked the same things and we were both in a graduate program at the same university for social work. She was like a carbon copy of me. We hit it off, and when I visited Jacine, I visited Sandra.

This day, Tammy was already at Sandra's and when she opened the door for me, the look Sandra gave me was more like hatred instead of our usual friendly greeting. Reluctantly, I walked in and playfully joked with Tammy, like we always did. Instead of our usual banter, she sat there with a look of confusion and fear, and Sandra matched her gaze as if I walked into some secret club they formed and interrupted them.

Tired of the foolishness, I called Tammy out. I said, "What did you do, tell her some sob story like you are the victim?" Tammy just sat there. Sandra felt the need to defend her (like I said, we were carbon copies) and I gently backed out of this fight. I was done fighting for Tammy, with Tammy and about Tammy.

Jacine was the one to help me understand what was going on. After I talked to her about the strange encounter I had with them, she talked to Sandra and she learned that Tammy had tried her best to assassinate my character. I couldn't believe the lies she told. She told Sandra that I wasn't there for her and that I'd never been a good friend. She said she moved here, but I abandoned her. She said that I didn't want to help her move. There were so many lies that I didn't have the energy to refute them. I knew that time would tell and that Tammy would show her true colours to Sandra, the same way she did with everyone else. It didn't take long before this came to pass, but by that time, I had moved on. I left Sandra and Tammy to deal with each other.

I distanced myself from Tammy. I was tired of the

emotionally draining relationship that we had. Quan said he saw a difference in me when we hung out and he didn't like it. I had begun to take on her problems and it caused tension in my home. She managed to get my attention by telling me that her youngest daughter was in the hospital for a procedure. I rushed to her side, as she knew I would. I hung out with her a few times after that, but I could never truly allow myself to trust her again.

In addition to everything else, when Berry assaulted my son, she remained friends with Debra. I never expected Tammy to confront Debra on my behalf, but she should have. That is what a friend would do. That's what I'd been doing our entire friendship. I met with her after she heard about my father's death, and we went swimming. It was good to see her. She is witty, smart and funny, but she's an unsafe person.

Later, I sent her a text message, expressing how I felt about her failing to fight alongside me during different situations in my life. I explained that I would have never left her to fight alone, but that we would stand side by side. I told her that sometimes the advocate needs an advocate, and whenever I looked up, I was always alone fighting my fight without her.

She replied that she didn't mean to hurt me and she didn't know what to do at this point. I expressed that I just wanted her to know how I felt. I thought she would get it better in a text, because she would have to listen to me and process it. The next day I received a text saying this wasn't about her being friends with Debra, nor was it about her, it was about my dad dying and she was just caught in the crosshairs. She still doesn't get it.

In essence, my mid-thirties brought about a change in my friendships like no other time in my life. These relationships were special to me and I would not be who I am without them. I hope that one day we all find the healing and closure that we need so that we can be kind to ourselves first of all, and secondly we can be kind and loving to others.

Befriending people as an adult is more difficult than it was for me when I was younger. One reason could be that I have standards and expectations now that I didn't have before. I hold myself and my loved ones accountable for their actions and I am not a blind supporter of mess. If you are wrong, you are wrong, period. I expect my friends to call me out and I hope they expect to be called out. I may not always agree with my friends beliefs, attitudes or behaviours, but we connect through our mutual respect for one another.

His Promise

A dishonest man spreads strife, and a whisperer separates close friends.

-   Proverbs 16:28

His Promise

I promise to trust the process and growth of my relationships and to accept wherever they end up.

CHAPTER 7

A Village

Daddy's Fall From Grace

I believe that God can restore relationships. As much as I loved my parents, it is no secret that I got along with my dad the most. We had our knock down drag out disagreements, but I was always respectful, and he was always practical and loving. I struggled with my parents' divorce for years, and my dad tried to reassure me that nothing would change, but it did. Everything changed.

Growing up a daddy's girl, I put my father on a pedestal that he never asked to be on. After my parents divorced, my dad moved within walking distance from our house and he was very active in staying in contact with me. When he moved to Alabama, I was devastated and I felt like the only one who understood and protected me was gone. During this time, I was sexually abused by my brother's friend while I was being physically, mentally and emotionally abused by my mom, but I kept on smiling. 'Nobody likes a cry-baby,' is what my mom and her friends would tell me. I needed an ally.

I would call my dad in the midst of these horrible things

happening to me and he would tell me to pray for my mom. I didn't want to hear that. I was a child and I needed him there to physically cover me - while she kicked, screamed and hollered at me - like he used to. Every summer he came to get me, and whenever he was able, he came when I called him.

As an adult, my dad and I remained close. He sounded lonely to me and his health wasn't what it used to be. I missed him, so my family packed up and moved to Alabama to be close to him. When I came here, I was hoping to find the man I grew up admiring, but the reality of it was that he was human. I guess I never noticed that about him; superman had lost his cape.

One disappointment after another: he wasn't there for me after my divorce or my second bout of homelessness. I needed support and he wasn't there for me. He missed my graduation and my second/last wedding. He had met someone new, and he was focused on making that work. He was a great father, but when it came to his love life, he was a bit too focused. Eventually, he remarried, and moved to Germany with wife number four and though

I loved him, I knew things would never be the same. My relationship with my dad changed, but because of him, I knew that God would never change.

As I said, my dad was everything to me while growing up. When I became an adult, he had his own life to live. When he died in 2015, I was 36 years old and he didn't owe me anything at that point. I was hurt, and this entry was written during a time when I missed him and felt that I needed him and he wasn't there. I was emotional when I wrote this and I felt alone. He did not approve of my marriage to Mitch, so no, he was not going to come here. With Quan, he gave us his blessing, but he was out of the country in Germany. I could have stayed at home here in Alabama I'm sure, but he had allowed three other people to live there and he couldn't put them out because I needed a place to stay for three days. This is what pain looks like, it distorts reality and we have to be fair when we tell our side of the story.

His Promise

For I, the Lord, do not change.

- Malachi 3:6

My Promise

I promise to set my expectations for my loved ones reasonably.

On Daddy's Deathbed

When my dad died in 2015, I was devastated. I had just visited him in Texas and he made it clear what his wishes were. When I received a text message from his last wife five hours after leaving him stating my dad died, I had a full break down. That's how I found out that my best friend, my protector, has died, in a text message. His wife had found the updated amended will and suspiciously he died right after that. I can't say what really happened, but I do know that God will handle it.

It left me grief stricken and grasping for answers concerning his last wishes. I received a general email with the promise of an inheritance, from a loved one so naturally I thought this was about my dad. He amended his will before he passed. Since then his last wife, number four, has avoided me and my brothers. She disagreed with the changes and disappeared. I should have known that this email was suspicious, but I didn't give it much thought.

They asked for my full name and requested that I reply to them via email. In my grief and desperation for answers,

I sent them what they asked for without first doing the research. I should have known better, since it didn't come from my lawyer, it wasn't on letterhead, and it did not have a telephone number attached. It caught me off guard, and that's what predators depend on.

This is common amongst takers. They see a vulnerable person, and may offer answers, support and comfort, but all they really want to do is take. People steal all type of things, my husband describes people who only want to waste your time as "time stealers" but I call them all, "takers."

One of the things that my dad left me that I didn't receive was his BMW. As a graduation present that same year, as a way to make it up to me, my husband Quan presented me with a white X5 BMW truck. He said, "Babe you didn't get the BMW your dad left you, but here you are from the both of us." I was so surprised and grateful that it made it that much easier to forgive his wife for all that she had stolen from me and my family. It was a process and it still took years to get beyond the point of having a physical reaction when her name was mentioned. I thank

God for forgiveness.

His Promise

The thief cometh not, but for to steal, and to kill, and to destroy: I am come that they might have life, and that they might have it more abundantly.

-   John 10:10

My Promise

I promise to allow God to curse those that curse me and bless those that bless me.

Mourning Mikey

I mourn the relationship that I wish I could have with Mikey. Loving a child with an attachment disorder is like loving a baby rattlesnake, the most venomous kind, because it can't control the amount of venom that it secretes. It would make more sense if he did not love to cuddle, hug and discuss his dreams with me. He would say, "I love you Mom," daily. He is receptive to my hugs, and affection often. I love this part of him. The soft parts, the sweet parts of him that I tried so hard to preserve and cultivate into a young man that would be the same to his wife and children one day. That boy is still here, but there are other parts of him that confuse me.

He would meet a stranger and wants to become part of their family. The boy who tries so hard to impress people that he will never meet again, but will abuse the very ones that love him. The parts of a boy that run away and make up elaborate stories to others- "I'm an orphan." "My mother beats me with sticks." "I don't want to live with my family." "I hate my family." "I want to live in the woods."

It's confusing, because I want him to fully be the loving child he can so easily portray one minute. Yet once he has been found by the police officers, the lies begin and he has gone so far as to say that he doesn't know me, in front of my face.

I find myself asking often, "Who is this child?" and praying, "Father, how can I help him to feel the love that I have for him, but more importantly, that you have for him?" He hurts the very ones who love him the most.

My love for Mikey is hardly returned and it's disheartening to say the least. I would see glimpses of a boy who desires love and affection, only to have him runaway, literally, no matter how much I love on him. It's amazing to see the transformation from one moment to the next. There are no external triggers. Nothing can make him stay or go. I used to think there was something that I was doing or was not doing.

I began consciously making extra time for him, we always talked, but we did science experiments, watched his shows together, played more games. I did his chores and continued to make sure he received the support that he needed from his therapists and school. I talked to Quan often about how he could "lighten up, and give him the benefit of the doubt more often." Nothing made a difference. He continued to steal from us, lie to us and on us, runaway and fail in school.

My actions toward him were not a variable in his behaviour. My support and empathy for him seemed to allow him to rebel even more. He did not go without discipline, we talked about his behaviour and came up with plans to do better next time. Sometimes he got a spanking, sometimes he got his electronics removed. Nothing changed him. He only adapted. Reward systems do not work with him either. There is no motivation to do something different. Why should he when he takes what he wants all of the time? Whether it was controlling my time, stealing my money, or manipulating others so that they are a part of this story of which he is the author and illustrator.

I read somewhere that biological children cannot have an attachment disorder, this article stated that it is found solely in foster or adopted children. So, this theory suggests that those children, had they stayed in their homes with their parents or other family members would not have an attachment disorder? I believe the same children that were removed from their homes would still have the same diagnosis. In my case, Mikey experienced trauma at a young age that altered his brain, but I did not give him up. I raised him and loved him through his pain.

Watching this beautiful boy wait for a dad who abandoned him, has been heart-breaking. I have to come to terms with the fact that my love will not fill this void. Mikey has learned to protect himself from being abandoned, by being the one who chooses to leave on his terms. He is in control of the separation, except the people that he hurts are the ones who stayed.

Attachment Disorder or not, children need to feel loved. They need to know that you love them and that you want them around. In my research I found that one way to help children with this particular disorder is to love them into submission. Basically starting from the beginning and doing everything for them that they did not get as an infant or toddler. This would not work in my case, since I cannot reverse the damage that his father did by abandoning him.

I never left Mikey, I have always been present. There is nothing that I could have done differently to change my reaction to the situation. So for my family, we have to address issues as they arise and move forward. We have to call on the Creator of love to fix this however He chooses. I am not sure which methods God will use to heal Mikey. It could be a number of things, but I know that He will turn things around for him and heal our family. All we need is God.

No matter what age I was when I had them, I made it a mission to let my children know how much I love them. By my mid-thirties, Mikey had completely changed the way that I viewed the love between a child and his mother. Unfortunately, variables play a part in our children not receiving or accepting that love. I can't imagine how difficult it has been for Quan to be in the midst of the crossfire, and sometimes the target of it. Mikey has physically hurt Jack several times.

The first time, Jack was six months old and Mikey was seven, he kicked him several times in his soft spot in order to make him disappear. I had only ran to the bathroom for a minute; it was the first time I left Jack alone after I found Mikey standing over him holding a pillow over his face when he was a few months old. This was Quan's son, being abused by his step son who made it clear by his actions that he hated him and everyone around him. Mikey's therapist tried several medications, but the medications didn't stop his desire to inflict pain on any of us. The first time Mikey admitted to poisoning me he was eight years old. Therapist's asked him if he was abused, neglected, if he felt alone or like we didn't care for him, he never expressed any of these concerns, which is why he remained in our home. They couldn't do anything, because Mikey was safe.

In hindsight, my expectations of Quan were unfair, he had always been there for all of us, he attended therapy and doctor's appointments, and never complained, even when he had to take off of work to pick up Mikey from school for threatening a student or teacher. He attended IEP meetings and interventions and advocated for him right beside me.

I wanted him to smile and be fluffy and soft and kind and to mask the way I was masking, but he couldn't. He is our protector and Mikey was hurting us all. He couldn't put a mask on and play video games with Mikey anymore. By the time Mikey was twelve, Quan had reached his breaking point; understandably so. Quan continues to provide for Mikey, but he has come to accept the fact that he is dangerous, something his therapist has been saying since he was six years old. I was the one in denial.

I did what I could considering my options. I couldn't put him outside and lock the door. I had a responsibility to Mikey, Jack and Quan. Quan has been the father, provider and protector for our family since day one, and I love and appreciate him more than he could ever know. I would have left me and Mikey a long time ago, if I were him. It was on the table a few times. He did consider leaving with Jack, in order to protect his peace. I didn't blame him and I couldn't stop him, but my wonderful therapist with the help of other organizations, put things in place to help our family.

His Promise

And we have known and believed the love that God hath to us. God is love; and he that dwelleth in love dwelleth in God, and God in him.

- I John 4:16

My Promise

I promise to do what is best for my family as a whole, whatever that looks and feels like.

Raising Hell for Mikey

My children know that when they need me, I will be right there. When I sat to write this, it was with a heavy heart because Mikey was being hospitalized. He was taken into police custody initially for trying to break his bedroom window and then setting a fire in his room after I told him that he had to stay there while I took a nap after a long day of work. I could not leave Mikey in the living room or in my room with me while I am asleep, for obvious reasons. Mikey does not appreciate structure and boundaries and in his true fashion, he did what he does best, create a distraction.

Once he was in police custody, he admitted to the police that he has been poisoning me by placing my toothbrush in the toilet, and rubbing it in between his buttocks amongst other things – his words not mine. They asked him what his intentions were and he stated that he wanted to kill me. This was not new to me, in fact, he has been telling people that he wants me dead for several years now.

The looks on the officers' faces was that of confusion and amusement. This child who they know very well, due to multiple interactions with him, is well taken care of. They see the motivational words for him on my walls; they witness the interactions between us; they see the love that I have for him and the way he mimics love with me, yet he wants to kill me. One of the officers stayed behind and left a pamphlet on Domestic Violence for me. He said that it was mandatory for him to leave this information, although he knows that we are well beyond what the pamphlet offers. I smiled and accepted the packet before walking him out.

After they took my son away in handcuffs I wondered how long he had been trying to kill me this time. I wish there had been some sign that he was doing this again. There weren't any signs, no triggers, no issues outside of the norm. He had been his normal self, full of hugs, kisses and defiance. It is a gumbo that I can never acquire a taste for. It does explain why I had been feeling so awful for a while. This was not the first time he had done this to me. I can't be sure that one day he won't succeed. Yet even though he has a plan to end my life, he still needs me.

He called me from the facility he was being held in. His breath sounded laboured and I asked him what was wrong. He said that he was having a hard time breathing. Mikey knows that no matter what, I will always have his best interest at heart. I asked him what the staff had done to help him. I already spoke to a nurse the night before about his asthma and so I was worried and anger brewed in the pit of my stomach. Mikey said that he was given two puffs from his inhaler. I asked him to put the nurse on the phone.

The nurse sounded guarded and annoyed and I used my polite, yet authoritative, voice to assure her that I was not questioning her abilities or telling her how to do her job. I expressed my concern and suggested that Mikey be given a nebulizer treatment. The nurse sounded even more offended and informed me that she already gave him a breathing treatment, his inhaler. I educated her about the difference between a breathing treatment and two puffs from an inhaler.

She told me that I could come and get my child if I wanted to, after I informed her that I may have to call the ambulance to get him if she wouldn't treat him. I told her that I will do just that, and I would be there soon if she did not feel that she can treat him there. I asked her if she was following protocol by requesting a parent of her patient to pick him up. She denied that she said that and stated that she would contact the doctor to check him again. I asked her to call me back to let me know whether I needed to come get "my child" or not.

She called me back 15 minutes later and stated that the doctor did not feel that he needed a breathing treatment. I asked what Mikey was doing. She said that he was playing, running around and laughing at the time and he was not showing any signs of distress at all.

I pictured Mikey smirking at the thought of me raising hell to care for him even then, after knowing that he wanted to kill me. The confusion I feel of love, fear and concern for his well-being was crippling. I would find myself becoming engulfed in his world, since it is impossible to bring him into mine.

I told myself that, perhaps, his hugs, kisses and constant, "I love you Mom's" were ways for him to manipulate me and keep me docile and unsuspecting of harm. Maybe he really wanted to feel this way about me, but there was something within him that wouldn't allow the love to reach me. Perhaps this was God's way of helping me to be able to care so deeply about him. His behaviour, absent of the bouts of affection he shows me would alienate me, even if it was a little bit. He still needs me, he was only 12 years old at the time and I was all that he had, besides God.

It was his way of making sure that I will always be here for him, even at his worst. I wonder what he will do if one day he succeeds in ending my life and I am no longer here. It's hard not to think this way, and I am not sure which thought bothers me more: Mikey being alone or him killing me and leaving his little brother, his sister, my grandbabies and his stepfather without me. I believe he will be alright, since he is able to adapt to any situation like a chameleon.

I realised though that I was the one who needed to change. He had the ability to move me like a marionette puppet. He tugged at my heart strings and I danced. I wanted to be free of this bondage as bad as I wanted him free of his demons. I prayed for deliverance and protection for all of us against harm.

Mikey has been in and out of facilities since this incident, this was a turning point in how I had to handle Mikey if I wanted us to be safe. I never imagined having a child of mine trying to kill me. When he looked me in my eyes and said, "Mom, I wish I cared, I want to care, but I can't. I can say I care. I can lie if you want me to," I felt that. I understand that these issues are out of his control and beyond any amount of help that I alone can provide him. He's fourteen now and this incident with the fire and poisoning happened two years ago. It wasn't the first time or the last. It's definitely been a journey of learning and healing.

How does one move on when the situation is still very present? My answer is that you don't. I have learned to lean into these cases where I want to show up for Mikey, and fight his battles, I do it when necessary and through prayer and meditation, I have learned to allow God to do His job.

Being a parent to a child with six diagnoses is a challenge, so is being the step parent and sibling. I thank God for the team of people that have been present for Mikey. It absolutely takes a village to help Mikey. His teachers, principals, school counsellor's, county workers, Madison Police Department and all of his mental health professionals have been a pivotal help in our family's healing process.

His Promise

You are from God, little children, and have overcome them; because greater is He who is in you than he who is in the world.

- 1 John 4:4

No weapon that is formed against thee shall prosper; and every tongue that shall rise against thee in judgment thou shalt condemn. This is the heritage of the servants of the Lord, and their righteousness is of me, saith the Lord.

- Isaiah 54:17

My Promise

I promise to remember to thank those who help me along the way.

Mother Matters

I had heard three different people told my 12-years-old son, Mikey, three different versions of, "I don't care what your mother says," three times in one week. Only to have them eat those words later. The first situation was Mikey's Junior Probation Officer (JPO) trying to exert his authority by discounting mine during our first meeting by telling Mikey, "Don't look at your mother, she can't say nothing about anything that is going to happen to you now." This was completely untrue, since there is no one in the world more equipped to give background information about a child than his mother who has raised him all his life.

I tried to keep an open mind as he used the scare tactic on a child that is not afraid of anyone, not even God. He also made empty threats which Mikey tested the very moment we left out of his office. What people fail to realize is that I am my children's first line of defence and when you discredit or discount me by telling them that I have no authority in their lives, it immediately removes our ability to work together to help them move forward and achieve their goals.

The next day after the meeting, Mikey told his JPO that he violated his probation and he was ready to get arrested. The JPO was completely floored since he thought that he would put fear in a fearless child. Had he chosen to work with me and read through the materials I gave him regarding Mikey, he would know what methods to use with him.

The second time was with my daughter, whose anger got the best of her. My daughter took issue with her brother stealing from her, this time he ate her cereal without permission. This would be okay if he used a bowl, or even washed his hands without being told. He would reach into the box with dirty hands and eat straight out of it. The box would then either be given to him or thrown away. She saw the box and the situation became heated.

She had a right to feel frustrated. I suggested that she have him do her laundry, clean up after her and/or any other form of recompense she felt, as long as it did not involve her hitting him. When I walked out of the room, I heard muffled noises. I returned to the room, where she had been choking him and hitting him in the face. Her reaction did not match the offense. When I confronted her, instead of taking my advice, she turned around to my son, her brother, and stated, "If you touch my stuff again, I am going to do much worse to you, and I don't care what anyone says." This was 100% disrespectful.

I had already spoken to Mikey, and offered to replace her cereal that he ate without permission. This behaviour removed any ability for us to work together as a united front. This was not the first time I told her to keep her hands off of her little brother. She forced my hand to make her choose between refraining from putting her hands on Mikey or moving out. She chose to move out the next day while I was at work.

The third time in a week was from my very own husband. Same child, different situation. Mikey had stolen the keys for the front locks that were installed to prevent him from running away on one of his many adventures. Quan found the keys in his pocket after I found him tampering with the lock. Mikey's finger was hurt during

Quan removing the keys from his hand. Although my heart literally aches when my kids so much as stump their toe, I said, "Oh well Mikey, you shouldn't have tried to run away." I saw his fingers; they looked fine.

Mikey has a way of making me take care of him instead of focusing on the issue at hand. I am aware of this. I told him to get ready to go. Quan walked into the kitchen during this exchange and began questioning Mikey about his actions. Mikey kept looking at me, and I chose to ignore him, because his stepfather was talking to him and it was not my place to intervene or answer for him. I kept packing my lunch for work. Quan became infuriated and belted, "Don't look at your mother, she is not going to do anything to me. I can do what I want to do to you, she can't stop me." This comment put me in a place where I had to once again defend my right as Mikey's mother.

I felt like I was being tested on every front to defend the very child that disobeys, disrespects and steals from me. I felt foolish in that moment, because here I was again in a triangle fighting for a child that wants nothing more than to sit back and experience the chaos that ensues when it is about him. I responded, "Look, you could have just kept this between you and him without putting me in it. I said what I needed to say to him earlier and my ignoring him was intentional. Now, instead of the focus being on what you were trying to accomplish, you turned this into a pissing match and it shouldn't be like this. I will not let you or anyone else abuse him, but you can teach him, discipline him and correct him." This turned into a huge argument and Mikey won.

Quan was not getting the reaction he wanted from Mikey, so he turned his attention to me. This happened often when I stepped back and allowed Quan to do his thing. Of course, then I was accused of not allowing him to have a voice in this relationship. I have tried to explain how triangulation works, but that goes out of the door in a moment.

As a 40 year old mother, I had paid my dues, and the last thing I wanted to feel was discredited or unimportant in my child's life. It's a God given right for parents to be a pillar in their children's lives and it's important that everyone respects that. I had been at the end of my rope by the time this incident occurred with Quan. After hearing Mikey's Junior Probation Officer, AJ and then Quan tell Mikey how unimportant I am as his mother, I felt disrespected to say the least. In wanting to reassure myself of my role in my child's life, I became assertive and angry. I was tired of being disrespected and no one had endured more than I have from Mikey. Quan has a right to feel his feelings as well, he has also been through hell with Mikey, but there is a way to express that without discrediting the other parent.

Parents are supposed to be a united front. In situations where both parents don't agree, these matters should be handled in a respectful and calm manner in front of the kids or privately the same way. My prayer is that we come together and respect each other's strengths and utilize each other for who we are, and what we do as a nurturer and disciplinarian, because we need both.

His Promise

Train up a child in the way he should go: and when he is old, he will not depart from it.

- Ephesians 6:1-4

My Promise

I promise to feel secure in who I am, without needing validation from anyone else.

The Wrong Counsel

One major flaw that I prayed to be delivered from was my habit of seeking confirmation from others, once God had already given me peace. This lack of faith came from the pain and struggle that I faced with my children and the people I loved the most. When I allowed the enemy into my thoughts, he was my accuser, so I began to feel punished. As a result, I questioned if God had forgotten me or even worse, if He despised me. If I allowed these thoughts to manifest, I would end up in a place where I felt worthless, unloved and unsure, which made it impossible to make even the smallest decisions.

AJ leaving while I was at work, after she assaulted Mikey for stealing from her left me devastated. Walking into my home, and not seeing or hearing her or the twins took me back to the first time she was taken from me. I wanted her with me. She knew this and it didn't matter. She chose to sneak out instead of having a discussion with me. I had already been through enough and this was the last straw. I couldn't allow this chaos to continue in my household. The liberty that people have taken with my emotions was no longer an option for them. Abandonment issues hit different when it's your kids that leave.

I contacted her that day. I informed her that she needed to call me to make arrangements to pick up the rest of her things.

She replied in a text four days later, "That's fine. I believe I have all the things that I need. Thanks."

Based on the information that I had at that time, I was well within my right to believe she did not need anything she left. I should not have made any other assumptions. It was something she had done before: leaving and not reaching out to let the family know that she was okay. She had left several expensive items that my friends had bought for her new-born twins and after I had not heard from her, I figured she had gone back to Connecticut. She did not have any friends in Alabama that I knew of at the time, so that text appeared pretty final to me.

I told my co-workers that I wanted my friends to pick up their gifts, some ranging up to about $100 (mostly baby swings and rockers). Buying them was a sacrifice for everyone, including myself. The bassinet that I had purchased for her was crammed in the closet with the rest of her unwanted belongings. My co-workers were floored at the thought of me not keeping the baby furniture in my two bedroom apartment in a room with my 12-year-old son, Mikey, for my grandbabies who I believed were one thousand miles away.

One said, "Yushima, she just needed a period to calm down; don't give away her stuff."

It was irrational for me to think that I should keep gifts that she abandoned, in my son's room, for my grandbabies that may be toddlers or school age by the time I saw them again. I could not convince her to see the rationale behind my decisions. She even said that she was "playing devil's advocate." Why would anyone try to be combative during a time like this? Why did I care? Why did I try to seek approval from someone who did not have any stakes in the situation? I was second-guessing myself. She was not aware of my history with my daughter and did not sit in on the prayers that I prayed.

Before I had left my house that morning, I had peace about whatever God placed on my heart, but then, I disturbed that peace when I made the decision to bring this understanding to others. I had to learn how to leave things at the altar.

His Promise

Blessed is the man that walketh not in the counsel of the ungodly, nor standeth in the way of sinners, nor sitteth in the seat of the scornful.

- Psalm 1:1

My Promise

I promise to protect my heart while loving others.

CHAPTER 8
No Might in Thine Hand

Being labelled as a Strong Black Woman has had its disadvantages; being labelled as strong minimizes my need and being Black takes away the authority that I would otherwise have over my children.

Although there were services that Mikey qualified for, he was often overlooked, because I was seen as that mom who had it all together, which could not be farther from the truth. The way I conducted myself and my education level allowed me to be prepared when seeking help for Mikey. It indicated that I had the strength needed to endure the sleepless nights spent searching for Mikey after he ran away. I looked like I could handle the early morning rush to work at 4:30 am, the false accusations and the sideway glances from my neighbours because the police were at my house at least 5 times a week about Mikey.

I had to deal with the violence he inflicted on his brother, the threats from my husband to leave and take my little one away from me, the medical issues I had, the stress, weight gain and the chest pain. I was not God and I needed him. I also knew that I needed help with my son, but when I told them what we were going through, they looked at me and told me how well I was handling it all. They informed me that as long as he was safe in the home, they couldn't assist me. I accepted that answer from the Department of Human Resources after I heard it for the fifth time. I decided to move forward and kept Mikey in counselling on my own, continued with the Individualized Educational Program and sought out resources on my own.

I later called DHR to close the case that I had opened with them after I came out, due to Mikey running away and making false allegations of abuse, in an unsuccessful attempt to get back to his dad. I was told by DHR that I could not close the case. Even though they could not help me with what I wanted, I could not close the case until they knew that I solved the issues that our family was having with Mikey.

They wanted to be onlookers into my already chaotic life, in order to assert control, without actually offering services that I had already established for him. They were apologetic, claimed to understand my situation and confirmed that Mikey was safe; but we were not safe with him in my home. They did home visits monthly, gathered data and even witnessed him sneaking out during our meetings. The worker was nice and caring, but she admitted that she could not help with anything else apart from what I had already established.

Whenever a solution presented itself, it was later removed due to some reason beyond their control. They could not provide the resources that my child needed, but they controlled whether or not I could close a case that I opened for my child. It basically gave them control over my entire family. God probably meant for it to be that way, so I just prayed.

This experience taught me that sometimes eliciting assistance can backfire. The challenges with Mikey mixed with the depression that had settled in my spirit from AJ leaving, trying to being loving and kind to a child that kissed me one minute and poisoned me the next, coupled with holding it together for my youngest son enough to make sure he understood that he was special and loved and being there for my loving husband was a bit much for me. In addition to working every day and seeing a high risk population of clients, it's safe to say that I was severely depressed. I was feeling every bit of the oppression that I suffered as a black woman in America who had brought someone else into our fold that did not mean us well.

Now I am proud to say that this situation has been resolved and the new caseworker that took over Mikey's case has been awesome and continues to work with our family and provide services as needed.

His Promise

Thy sons and thy daughters shall be given unto another people, and thine eyes shall look, and fail with longing for them all the day long; and there shall be no might in thine hand.

- Deuteronomy 28:32

My Promise

I promise to trust the process and know that God's in control.

My Arrest

The day I got arrested, I knew I had reached a breaking point. I was arrested for protecting my children and charged with Domestic Violence/Harassment of a Family Member and bailed out by people who I didn't think could care less about me. Life is funny that way. The irony of my arrest was that I was protecting my child from my overworked and over tired husband who had a chip on his shoulder that night. I allowed him to discipline and try things his way, but 30 minutes later, when the crying did not stop and my nerves had gotten the best of me, I went in to deescalate the situation. Things went terribly wrong and I became the enemy.

The brunt of his venomous words stung my soul and it was pure chaos. The attack came swift and unexpected, then I found myself defending all of my children at once, even my daughter who wasn't there. He called them names and rattled on about how terrible of a mother I was to have such f*cked up children. One child was called a whore and the other one was crazy as hell. He made remarks about my mother and unravelled my entire life before my eyes as easily as if it were a piece of yarn from a sweater that had been snagged.

He stood as close as he could and yelled that I was just like my mother. But I was confused because my mother never protected me. I did not understand and I couldn't believe the words he was yelling at me, all because I wanted to calm my baby down. I knew he was upset at this. However, when I failed to talk him down, in the midst of the assassination attempt at my character, I called him an a**hole.

I swooped up my five-year-old who happened to be caught in the middle of this war that he didn't sign up for and I ran into my room. Mikey was in his room and he was out of harm's way - physically anyway. I wanted it to stop but when Quan pulled on Jackson's tiny fragile arm to take him from me, I lost it. He continued to spit out venomous hate and I provided the bite. He threatened to call the police and I saved him the trouble and called them myself. The part of me that was hurting wanted to be punished and I wanted to punish him for hurting me as well. I only ended up hurting myself worse.

I knew I had to do something extreme in order to stop what was happening at that moment, even if it meant that I would be arrested for domestic violence. My husband gave his side to the very polite and kind officers on the scene and even showed them his bruise. I, on the other hand, covered all of mine because there was no need for both of us to be arrested and have my children in foster care.

I explained to my boys that I had been a bad mommy and was going to jail for a little while because I was not aware of the 24 hour hold until after I had spoken with the police. My little one was devastated, asking me to apologize so that I did not have to go. I apologized to Quan and my boys and explained that our actions had consequences; there were no excuses. My heart sunk when he looked up and asked me, with tears falling from his big doe eyes, "Who is going to kiss me Mommy? If you go to jail, who will kiss me?"

I explained that I would kiss him enough right then to last him until I returned and he cried.

The officer allowed me to slip out while Mikey entertained him. Mikey was fine with my arrest and did not show anything but excitement at the entire ordeal.

I looked at my husband before they took me and I wondered if I had made a huge mistake. He showed no remorse, no interest and no concern for me. I was not sure what I expected or wanted from him at that time, so I guessed my feelings of abandonment were not justified. I knew that something was terribly wrong in my home and I needed to fix it by any means necessary.

I passed the time in jail by reflecting on what I was doing with my life and made a plan to change before I messed it up even more. I did not call anyone. I only spoke to God and my bunkmate the last three hours that I was there. During that time, I realised that I had become complacent in the mess that I had made of my life and that was not okay. I built up walls too high to let pain in, but I couldn't let love, joy, peace, happiness or faith in either. I needed something drastic to happen. I had to start getting in-tune with my feelings. Jail plans didn't usually last, but I knew that I had to do something or I would lose everything.

My co-workers bailed me out 24 hours later; yes, that was embarrassing, but sweet. They came through before Quan could. He did pay for my bail; they just beat him to the punch.

We went to court and the detective recommended that the case be dismissed, since it was an isolated incident. Quan stated that he would not press charges and asked the judge to throw the case out. The judge could not do anything with the case until the next month, so I was awaiting trial and learning to be hopeful and proactive in preventing things from happening to me. I had to be in line with God's plan or my life would continue to be one huge earthquake after another. I was tired of rebuilding and it was time that I protected what I already had.

My arrest was my rock bottom. I knew then that if I wanted to be happy, I had to do better and learn how to handle my emotions. The fight between Quan and I was a culmination of the stress from our day to day duties, coupled with frustration and a lack of communication. We were both wrong and honestly we should have handled that entire situation better. I accept my role in it, and I had to live with the humiliation of being arrested and staying in jail for at least 24 hours. I wish I could say that I was anything but numb. That's where I was emotionally at the time. I was numb. Just when I thought life couldn't get any worse, it showed me otherwise. It's been two years ago, almost to the day that I'm writing this and all of the charges were dropped.

His Promise

The LORD thy God in the midst of thee is mighty; He will save, He will rejoice over thee with joy; He will rest in His love, He will joy over thee with singing.

- Zephaniah 3:17

My Promise

I promise to remember this experience, and never to duplicate it.

The Lies We Tell

Before my arrest, I had already begun questioning how realistic I had been while dealing with issues in my life. I had been coping with my abrasive life by becoming numb but I felt like a Stepford Wife without the perks. I found myself putting out fires all around me and not allowing myself time to bandage my third degree burns. I just kept on going. Unfortunately, becoming numb removed the ability to check in, so I was getting fatter, sadder and more detached from reality. I wondered how I was able to go to work, listen to my patients' problems, give great feedback and come up with plans. I was still genuinely caring towards them even though I was literally running on fumes.

In my search for truth, I had to ask myself some tough questions. I wondered if my obsession with my kids was natural or neurotic or if the gaping hole I felt when my boys were not in my home, even if they were at school, was normal. I felt an overwhelming sense of doom whenever I thought of anyone I loved and I lived in a state where I expected the worst to happen. Maybe it was because I didn't deserve to be happy or because I felt like God really had it out for me. Both thoughts were lies but the mind was a tricky thing.

In order to deal with the shift in my relationship, due to external factors and internal issues with both my husband and I, I created a dialogue in my mind about how much he loved and cared for me. I told myself and I told him how wonderful he was to me because I wanted to believe it, even though his actions and lack of empathy for me, as well as his disdain for Mikey said otherwise. It was mental illness 101.

In moments of clarity, I found myself questioning why I continued to live as though my son didn't hate me and wanted me dead. I wondered why I was taking my boys out, having a grand old time playing laser tag, bowling, video games and seeking family fun nights, when I knew it would only come to bite me in the butt; sometimes even before we made it back home. In lucid moments, I thought about the stories I created in my mind, as if I was watching someone else live out the lie and I figured that I must be bat crap crazy to carry on in that manner.

I knew why I did it. The truth hurts. I had so many people around who inflicted pain upon me that I couldn't bear another moment of loss and emptiness. I wanted to escape into a world of normalcy. I was not asking for unicorns or for my dad to reappear and hug me or tell me that things would be alright - those things are impossible. However, I could imagine a husband who not only loved me, but genuinely cared about my feelings. I could concoct a perfect blend of a protector and a nurturer.

When I took Mikey out and he was having a good time, he became the son who loved me back. In those moments, I was not locking doors or hiding toothbrushes; I was not worried about open waters being poisoned or lies being told about me. I became a mom and he loved me. When we were out having fun, Jackson was just my little boy and I was not worried about him no longer wanting me much like his siblings did. In those moments, I pictured him being "normal" and always wanting me around.

When I closed my eyes, my mother was never abusive; she had always given me advice and love and she had always shown concern for my well-being. I could imagine my daughter as a girl who needed her mother, and whose innocence was not taken by sick, perverse people. When I rewrote my history, my brother never helped my mother kidnap my daughter and he did not lie to me for months about her whereabouts. In my mind, my fictional story was always better than my biography. I was normal and more importantly, I was loved.

I wanted to see the spoils of my labour of love that I did for my family. I desired their love and concern. I wanted to be the best parent, wife, daughter, friend and counsellor that I could be. Before all of that was possible, I had to be the child in Christ that He created me to be. If I was lacking, I prayed that God revealed it and I claimed His promise of Him making me a virtuous woman.

It's common for someone under extreme duress to create a more palatable narrative. I found myself doing this for years. I created an alternate reality, in order to cope with my reality. How can a parent continue to be loving and kind to a child that tries to kill them and talks about it freely, without switching things up? I didn't split, that's another form of detachment, that occurs to create distance between the situation and the person in crisis. I can honestly say that my family was in crisis at this time. We were in constant fight and flight mode and it had taken its toll on us all in different ways. Two years later, Quan and I are in a much better space, emotionally. Mikey continues to be in and out of inpatient facilities and is in one now. Jack is a healthy, happy, loving seven year old boy that still loves his mother. I am blessed.

His Promise

[11] The heart of her husband doth safely trust in her, so that he shall have no need of spoil. (15) She riseth also while it is yet night, and giveth meat to her household, and a portion to her maidens. (28) [28] Her children arise up, and call her blessed; her husband also, and he praiseth her.

-    Proverbs 31: 11, 15, 28

My Promise

I promise to take an emotional inventory of myself and check in with my loved ones often.

Being There For Quan

I have recently learned to become more vulnerable. I am not sure if this was actually a conscious decision or the mere fact of my cheese sliding off my cracker and my inability to conceal my crazy. Whatever the case, when I feel like I need someone to help me through the hard times, I think about my father. My father was always my soft place to fall. I remember feeling that way with Quan when we first got married, and then life got real and the rug was pulled from under my feet.

We can handle just about anything when it involves "them" against us, but when a cog within our family system is broken, it destroys the entire infrastructure and at the time I could not expect support from my very supportive husband. He was in pain and broken, we were learning how to survive. I am a communicator, I love to communicate. I am the Communication Queen. I check in with my husband often, seeking to learn his feelings about things and following his final decision as gold within our home. I value him. I value his feelings. I value his opinion.

One thing Quan cannot deal with is my vulnerability. Whether it is my depression, or a need for him to be there for me emotionally, even a panic attack made him freak out, because he was not used to me being anything other than "together." He tends to see my need as a deficit on his part and internalizes my lacking as me accusing him of not doing something right. It turns into me ultimately trying to comfort him and validate his feelings. I end up feeling worse and I have shared less and less of my feelings with him for fear of the repercussion of an argument in the midst of my pain.

This had been a pattern for years. Therapy would help if we went together more often. I believe these behaviours are fixable. We even had a breakthrough once. He admitted, "Look, I just don't know what to do when I see you like that, I am used to you being strong, handling things." Seeing me "like that" means seeing me in any other state than smiling and happy, even if it is not authentic.

"Grin and bear it" has been my way of coping with everything since I was young. If something happened to me (rape, bullying, abuse), I found myself concealing my truth in order to prevent others from feeling uncomfortable. I never felt safe giving someone access to my secrets. When I did, I could expect them to be used against me, misunderstood or minimized and forgotten. My feelings never mattered to anyone but my father, and even him, in his humanity, could not always be there for me. When I am feeling completely alone, I know that I can always count on the Lord.

At the time that I wrote this, Quan had reached his wits end with Mikey and like me, the stress had began to show its head. For me it was depression, for Quan it was impatience and the fear that things were out of control to the point that it began to affect me mentally. Depression is a lonely disease and it whispers things into our psyche that will have us believing that we are all alone and no one cares about us.

Later when things calmed down, Quan and I discussed these issues, and I gained a better understanding of his point of view and sometimes he does not have the words to express his feelings, but when I give him time and space, he usually comes and clarifies things pretty well. He was afraid, and I was in pain, there wasn't anything that he could do about it. He was in pain as well, but he didn't express that, so it came out in the form of anger and frustration. We had not been to therapy for our relationship, at the time the only one receiving the most support was Mikey, but we were all suffering.

I commend Quan for sticking it out with us. Two years later, we are in a different space and we are learning to communicate better. I can't expect him to have the same communication style as I do. I have to do better when it comes to the expectations I place on him. He's allowed to have an off day, or an off week, hell an off month with all of the mess we've been through.

His Promise

I looked on my right hand, and beheld, but there was no man that would know me: refuge failed me; no man cared for my soul.

- Psalm 142:4

My Promise

I promise to be patient and understanding with my husband.

Being Strong for Them

"I am unapologetically broken. I am sick of being labelled by others. I am tired. I am hurt. I am lost. I don't have all of the answers. I have contemplated suicide. I love too hard. I change my mind too much. I am tired of fighting for everything, all of the time. I hate it when people call me strong. I am not strong. I am but a speck and lately on my good days, I am mediocre at best.

"As a Black woman, people use words to compliment me like, resilient, strong, brave, capable, independent and other adjectives that implicate that I don't need others to hold me up when all I want to do is fall from the weight on my shoulders that I never asked for. Strong people don't need help, they persevere and they fall through the cracks broken and sometimes unfixable. I believe I used to be strong. Now I am numb. I have been vulnerable, ignored, harassed and abused by every system available to me.

"I am not supposed to be soft and express my needs to others. I am expected to hold in my anger and hide my mental illness. I am supposed to bury my past and never seek justice for myself, my children or my husband. I am expected to be everyone's comic relief and personal counsellor. I am the mother for the motherless and the father to the fatherless. I make other people feel good about themselves, while they leave me empty and depleted. I should not expect a Prince to come and save me, I am expected to saddle up my horse and save everyone else.

"The Princess that Disney chose to represent me was a frog, and her god is not my god. I am my own blueprint, but others read me through their stereotypes. No matter how loud I scream, they muffle my cries with their right hand over my mouth, and their left hand on my neck, raping me with their own needs, while using my blood for lubrication.

"I am not an anomaly. I am a woman: fearfully and wonderfully made. I don't have to be strong. I am allowed to be delicate. It has taken me decades to realize that I need others. I am not a victim, but I am often victimized. I do not have the luxury of taking time off of work for exhaustion or checking myself into the hospital to process all that life has abandoned in my wake."

This is a direct entry taken from my journal. I was in the midst of a suicidal ideation, I just wanted to have peace. Life had taken its toll and I was tired of the expectations that the world placed on me. I was tired. I felt despondent and alone. I was in so much pain emotionally and physically. My labs were off, I was having hormonal issues and I wasn't taking care of myself. I needed a break.

My sister, Nubi, was here for me like no other. She knew that I was at my very end. She called and checked on me daily, she sent texts and words of encouragement. No one really knew how bad it was except her. She knew that I had made a plan, written letters and I was ready to end it all. I felt like my family would be better off without me. Again, depression is a liar and when it told me to end my life, it sounded so good to me at the time. I really had to fight for my life, every day that I woke up, I had to fight to stay alive. Living with Major Depressive Disorder and Chronic Fatigue Syndrome as well as other health issues brought me to my knees.

Finally, I talked to my doctor and she prescribed a mild antidepressant, I began taking my daily vitamins and treating my hormonal issues. I focused on what I could change, and I left everything else to God. I began praying more and meditating every morning before I did anything else. I had to stay here. My children and my husband needed me. My sister saved my life, and I can never repay her. Things didn't get better for me at this point yet, after the arrest, I knew I had to do something different, if I wanted something different.

If you have a friend or family member that suffers from depression, please check on them. It may become daunting sometimes because they are stuck in a loop of utter sadness, even if things appear to be good. The last thing you want to say to them is that things can be worse, and don't compare their life with someone else's who is doing worse.

If you suffer from depression, please seek medical and mental health assistance. My depressive symptoms were also compiled with the medical issues I had.

I wake up every day, and I thank God. I thank Him for not listening to my prayers when I begged Him to end my life. I am not always strong. I am fully human and fully dependent on my Creator for every breath, sometimes lacking the very will to live. Today, I am alive, and I look at my seven-year-old's big brown eyes and I couldn't imagine not waking up to them every morning, seeing my husband or hugging Mikey again. I would miss out on so much. What if AJ and I were to come together again, or if my mother and I figure things out? If I give up, there are no second chances.

His Promise

The LORD is my strength and my shield; my heart trusted in him, and I am helped: therefore my heart greatly rejoiceth; and with my song will I praise him.

-   Psalm 28:7

My Promise

I promise to listen to my body, mind and spirit and give it what it needs.

CHAPTER 9

Losses and Gains

Getting fired from my counselling job came as a surprise and a blow to my already somewhat fragile and deflated ego. My supervisor, who had a personal vendetta against me, received her last big hurrah before she was fired from her job. Every counsellor at the clinic had to complete the licensure or the Alcohol and Drug Certification within a two and a half year period.

The test was about $700.00 and from what I understood, it was fairly easy, so I did not worry about it. When it was time for me to take the test, this supervisor convinced me to take the Advanced Alcohol and Drug Certification, since I was a Master Level Social Worker: this would be a better fit for me. She was kind enough to provide study tools and encouragement, assuring me all the while that it was difficult, but worth it in the end.

By the time my new supervisor found out that I paid for and scheduled the test, it was too late to change to the regular test, with only two days before my scheduled time. He and the Program Director tried their best to help me with the test, but nothing could have been done to correct the mix up. A friend and co-worker of mine had called out my ex-supervisor, stating that she did not trust her motives and opted to steer clear of any advice she had to offer. My need to do the "right thing" motivated me to take the AADC instead of the ADC, since that was the "proper" test for an MSW.

Needless to say, I studied the materials she provided and purchased those that she suggested. In the end, it all proved to be futile as none of the materials I studied were for the much easier ADC that all of the other counsellors had taken. My ex supervisor had just taken the test and was well aware of this fact. On purpose she had advised me to study the wrong material.

I was later informed that only senior counsellors should attempt the AADC, since one needed to have been in practice for at least a decade to have the knowledge that it takes to pass it. I was a novice at the two and a half year mark, so I missed passing the test by six points, which was not so bad, considering.

The Program Director and my patients were sad to see me go, as well as my co-workers, that I now consider my friends. I was assured that I could come back at any time once I passed the correct test. I told them that I would take them up on that offer, but the more I thought about my future, the idea of staying in Alabama had become less appealing to me - I desired new opportunities.

I was shocked and surprised that I did not pass the AADC but I was disappointed. Thank God I was in a better space emotionally, because it wasn't a breaking point for me. I accepted that change is inevitable and I needed to go with the flow. Being unemployed was a difficult two months for me, and I am sure it was hard for Quan to handle all of our financial needs as well. We have both been in the position to have to "hold it down" for short periods of time when either of us found ourselves between jobs.

His Promise

I know your works. Behold, I have set before you an open door, which no one is able to shut, I know that you have but little power, and yet you have kept my word and have not denied my name.

- Revelation 3:8

My Promise

I promise to accept change as it comes without grumbling or complaining.

Dream Job in Florida

One week after losing my job and being denied unemployment for what they called a voluntary resignation, I received a call from the Program Director. He was excited to tell me that corporate contacted him as they were interested in interviewing me for a Clinical Training Specialist Position in Florida. They had no idea that I had been let go but they didn't care either way. They wanted me to come as much as I wanted to go.

For the first time in a long time, I felt like I was allowed to be happy about something for myself. My heart swelled with hope as the PD explained how impressed they were when corporate had visited and interviewed my patients. They were blown away by what was shared with them by my group. I had no idea that they had considered me at all.

I remembered meeting with one member of corporate two years prior, for this very position that was not yet open. I wanted it so much after visiting Florida and while going through the training myself, I knew it was the career path for me. I asked her to keep me in mind, and there we were, two years later, like Joseph and the baker that had forgotten him until God's perfect timing. I could hardly believe it, especially since the salary was almost double what I was making at the time. I had given up this dream after my arrest and all of the time that had gone by, but God remembered. He always remembers.

Crying and overwhelmed with joy, I ran to my husband to tell him the news. Our lives were about to either change for better or we could stay stagnant. We had toyed with the idea of moving to Florida before and he was on board then, so I didn't think it would be too hard for him to see that this was a move that our family would benefit from. It was a sign/gift straight from the Most High. However, I didn't want to pressure him or push him in either direction, so I gave him the information, prayed with family and friends and waited.

In order to make the process a bit easier for him, I presented him with job, housing and school options in Florida whenever I could. I made sure not to give him too much information to allow him to think about it and pray on it himself. It had to line up for us both if this was going to work.

When I received the call with my flight and hotel arrangements, it became real for me. I asked him if he had made a decision and he stated that he was still thinking about it. I answered all his questions and informed him that my cousin assured me that he had options for employment there. She was working for Disney and her husband drove trucks locally, so they would help him get a job without any issues. I remembered my husband telling me that he would like to drive trucks locally and as such, I could hardly contain my excitement.

I was all set to leave in a few days when I spoke to his daughter, who was really my daughter in spirit, and she informed me that he told her he wasn't planning on going to Florida at all. I asked him about this and he admitted to saying it to her, but not really meaning it; he assured me that I should go on my trip and remain positive. I was shaken at his admission and urged him to tell me the truth as I would have preferred to stay there instead of going to Florida; it would be a waste of time and resources. He promised me that I had his blessing, we prayed together then I went to Florida to meet my new co-workers and learn more about my new job.

I made it to Florida and my excitement during the entire process never wavered. It bubbled up and out, maybe too much during the interview, which possibly made me appear self-assured and possibly too friendly. The first day was a meet and greet and day two had the presentation, logistics and feedback. I asked for honest feedback and I was told what I had thought in the first place. The interviewer was concerned about my ability to deliver what they needed, because of my laid-back demeanour on day one, which came off as unprofessional to her I guess. However, she said that she was extremely impressed with my presentation and admitted that it was best she had ever seen in her five years of employment there.

I was disappointed in myself for being too relaxed on day one, but I was excited that I redeemed myself on day two. Then came the punch in the gut - they needed someone to start the following week. She actually stated that they needed someone yesterday and I was sure my face said everything that my heart felt. I thought I would have at least a month or two but I was advised that they did not have time to go back and forth. She stated that another candidate would be interviewed the following Monday, and I would hear from her then.

I decided that the job was mine. I needed it and I had not felt this feeling of hope, excitement and peace about a decision in several years. It was mine and I needed to make it work.

I waited for several hours before I called my husband to tell him the news. I needed to keep this feeling just in case things did not work out on his end. Despite my wanting to talk about it, he wanted to wait to discuss it face to face and I agreed.

That discussion never happened. He and the kids picked me up from the airport. My plane was late, I was tired and so was he. He remained laxed and unexcited about the news about work but he was happy to see me. I didn't want to argue, and I wanted him to bring it up but he didn't. He went to work the next morning and I texted him the following afternoon, asking for his decision. Like I thought, he had never planned on moving to Florida. My husband allowed me to go through the motions, knowing all along that it would never happen for me. I was devastated.

I tried to rationalize the reasons God would allow this to happen: to have something that I want so bad, come into my grip, only to take it away. Maybe the job was never mine in the first place. Maybe they didn't like me as much as they stated and what I saw as the stars lining up in my favour was really an arrow meant to pierce my heart. They would have to hire someone else; someone that was not me. I emailed them to thank them for their time and I wished them well in finding the right trainer for the position. My heart sank as I typed every word.

I decided to put it behind me and act like I was okay, since that was the only way I was accepted by my awesome, yet, avoidant husband. I decided to smile, and continue to kiss him hello and goodbye. I would cook, clean, take care of the children and find another job, here in Alabama. The whole experience was placed behind me.

I still had no idea why that happened, but it seemed I was meant to learn something from it. I wanted to be open to the lesson and I prayed that bitterness and resentment did not come into my heart. I wanted to be content wherever God placed me, even if I had to stay where I was at that time.

I was still very hurt when I wrote about this experience two years ago. It was still fresh and I remember my fingers shaking as I wrote about it. All of that emotion was real and raw. Of course, I have since forgiven Quan and I have moved on, but at the time, whew, I was thirty eight hot, as my friend Sherri would say.

Not accepting my dream job in Florida was very difficult for me. It took several months of prayer for God to remove the bitterness and resentment from my heart. At the time it was the only good thing happening to me and I had to turn it down for my family. A family that I felt didn't want me around anyway. It was a very confusing time for me. I love my husband and I wanted him to make this sacrifice for me, and although he didn't, I still believe that what was supposed to happen, happened. If that job was for me, we would have been on one accord and if Quan was being disobedient to what God wanted for us, God would have still moved mountains to make it happen.

His Promise

Trust in the Lord with all thy heart and lean not to thy own understanding, but in all thy ways, acknowledge Him and He shall direct thy paths.

- Proverbs 3:5-6

My Promise

I promise to forgive and move forward from disappointment without malice in my heart.

Quan Tripping About Money

Two months had passed since I stopped working, and one month since I passed on the opportunity to accept my dream job in Florida. I did all that I could to save our family money: from couponing, visiting three different stores to catch specific items on sale, to going without supplements, vitamins, prescriptions and/or certain foods that I would usually buy.

I asked Quan daily what he wanted to eat, what he wanted me to buy and what he had a taste for. He hardly ever knew and usually ends up eating what I prepare or just picking up something that he preferred. I had to be a mind reader, all the while knowing that no matter what I buy or what I do, it would be wrong in his eyes.

Living in an environment where my emotional needs weren't being met, small things became big and remained unresolved. On the verge of a panic attack, I practiced ways to ask my husband for items that would equal about $25.00, instead of asking for both. I was afraid to ask for anything. The tension in the house was so thick it was suffocating.

As I sat next to my sick six-year-old, who I kept home, I wondered what we were teaching him with my tears and his father's super frugal ways. It must have been confusing to see us smiling and having discussions one moment as equals and the next moment, his mother was being scolded like a teenager for asking for money. In those times, I pictured myself alone with my boys, living a healthy and fulfilled life, free from having to deal with the daily drama of begging my husband for a few dollars here and there.

I always respected my husband as the head of our family. If power tends to corrupt, I placed myself in a position to be mistreated, disrespected and discarded as a wife, mother and helpmate. I had to change the dialogue that I was having with myself and tried to remember who I am. My depression, coupled with the stress and lack of money was not a fun place to come home to.

I had to look back at this time to see the narrative when it came from places of hurt and insecurities. Being unemployed was scary for me plus I was obviously still pissed about the Florida situation and whenever I had to ask him for money, I would think, "You know what, I wouldn't have to ask you to for anything if I had taken the job." For a while, my journal entries were filled with anger about this financial stress our family was under.

I hadn't been in this situation in eight years and I was not happy about being placed on a budget that did not take care of our basic needs. I felt like I was being punished. It did not feel fair and I didn't know if our marriage would stand it. It was only two months, but that was a long two months of going without medication and basic needs. I know Quan was under a lot of stress himself, so that part is forgiven, but I will never understand why he treated me the way that he did during that time. That hurt me badly and I believe it changed my view of our marriage in some ways. I pray that we never find ourselves in a situation like that again, but if we do, I pray that we are understanding, patient and kind to one another.

His Promise

God is within her, she will not fall.

-    Psalm 46:5

My Promise

I promise to be mindful of my loved ones' feelings, even when I am stressed.

Pressure Over Peace

My brother convinced me to call my mother by using an age-old tactic: guilt. I had already been thinking about her and wondered if she was okay, but I had made a decision to move forward in my life. The loss of our relationship brought with it a peace knowing that I would no longer be responsible for making a toxic environment palatable for me.

I called her and although she had caused me unspeakable pain and loss in my life, my heart leapt at the sound of her voice. Her excitement and surprise could be felt as well. We had a good conversation and I realised that I missed hearing her laughter and her day to day going ons. However, I knew that in order to maintain my peace, I would have to continue to enforce the healthy boundaries of little to no contact.

The truth was that I missed my mother. I missed the relationship that we should have had, missed calling her and laughing at her unmatched witty conversations. Most of all, I missed the way she could make me feel like she cared about me and actually loved me. These things were usually temporary until the shoe dropped when my guard was down and I ended up at the brunt of a controversy or drama that I never knew existed. I always end up losing big when gambling with the desire to receive love from my mother. I learned to acknowledge what I felt and I have to believe what I know.

I used to confuse selfcare with unforgiveness. But then, my decision to create healthy boundaries was helpful in the healing process from the pain of my abusive past with my mother. I had to admit to myself that my desire to connect with her would never change who she was at her core and I had to weigh the price of talking to her with the effect it could have on my mental health.

I chose to simply check in but still kept my distance. I would allow God to do His job in us and if He saw fit to reunite us, He and only He would be the one to give me peace about our reunion. Until then, I would continue to pray for our healing and salvation individually.

No matter what she has done, I still love her and I will always want what's best for her. I want things to be different, but it's not what I want, it's what's real. I have to accept things the way that they are. I hope that one day we will be able to really come back together healed and complete, but it will have to be God who brings us together again, not my emotions.

His Promise

Let all that you do be done in love.

-    1 Corinthians 16:14

My Promise

I promise to love my mother and respect the space we
both need to continue to heal.

Peace Over Pressure

The very next day, after I called my mother, I received a call from my daughter, AJ. I was shocked and I was sure my silence conveyed the sheer surprise of it all. My mother had reached out to her and said that I must be up to speaking to both of them. This was the farthest thing from the truth, because no one stole my peace quite like AJ. The first words out of her mouth were, "Do you want me to drop them off to you? You don't have to speak to me, if you don't want to."

I asked her how she was doing and she explained that she could use some help and wasn't sure why we haven't spoken. (Red Flag #1) I reminded her that she asked me not to contact her ever again and I was abiding by her wishes. I wanted to understand what was happening with her, so I listened as she explained. She said that when other people asked where I was, she had to explain that I lived in Madison, but I wasn't talking to her and wished that we did speak. (Red Flag #2) I asked her why her grandmother/my mother hadn't moved in with her as planned and she stated that she believed my mother didn't want to leave her things there. It was also said that the task of moving right now was too great for her.

The part of me that wanted to swoop in and tell her to bring them over was hushed when she continued to speak. She asked me if I remembered our last conversation and I told her I did. My daughter continued to say that I told her that I was going to introduce her daughter, my grandbaby, to a thirty year old man when she turned ten years old. (Red Flag #3) I knew at that moment that she had not changed and her desire to gain sympathy from others by making up lies about me was always going to be a thorn in our relationship. The scary part was that she believed her own lies. I explained to her that I did not say that, nor would I ever say that and she must have misunderstood or misheard something.

After a while, I did not have the energy to continue to refute the allegation, so I left it at that. I asked her why she would trust someone with her child after a threat like that. She stated that she knew I would never hurt either of her kids or do anything to cause them harm. I then asked her to think about that and to apply that to the things that I would and would not say as well.

I would have loved to see my grandbabies as my heart ached at the loss that I feel without them. However, I had to ask myself what the price of seeing them and interacting with AJ would eventually cost me. I couldn't imagine the lies that she would tell on me if she were to become angry or bored. I couldn't risk it, so I chose my peace over pressure. She would never understand how her lies and behaviours continued to hurt me and I hoped she never experienced what I did as her mother. My prayer for her is that the Most High blesses her and her little ones and keep them safe from hurt, harm and danger; I pray that He provides their needs, whatever they may be.

His Promise

A lie against someone is like a dangerous weapon.

-    Proverbs 25:18

My Promise

I promise to continue to love and pray for AJ.

Perks

I received a call for an interview at a non-profit mental health facility. The job held the same title as my last, but the pay was lower and instead of working from 5:00 am to 1:30 pm Monday- Friday, I would be working from 8:00 am to 8:30 pm, twice a week and 8:00 am - 5:00 pm, twice a week with Fridays off unless there is a training. The pay would be an adjustment and the hours would be a sacrifice. I loved being home for my boys when they got home from school; it was a perk that I looked forward to. The debriefing of their day, snack time and the comfort of knowing they were safe and sound within my reach were very important to me. The hours that I would have to be away from my boys gave me pause.

When the Human Resource Representative called to offer me the position, I negotiated the salary, hoping to buy time before accepting. I had to find a safe and reliable person to watch my boys. Who would be up to such a task? How could this possibly work with me making less money? Those thoughts and so many more came to my mind. Bible verses that usually brought me peace, did not comfort me and my anxiety was through the roof, even after prayer. I knew this would be a necessary sacrifice.

The HR Rep called me back and explained that upon my completion of a certification, there would be a raise, and after working for ten years with them, my student loan debt would be forgiven. I perked up and stated, "You should have lead with that," and we both laughed.

I accepted the position, not because I felt at peace about missing time with my boys, but because the benefit of the position would eventually outweigh the cost.

I often found myself in positions where the payoff comes much later than the sacrifice. The pain of loss and betrayal often brought comfort in the form of peace that was rewarded when the healing process began.

I have been truly blessed to find a job that I enjoy. I loved my last job at the clinic and this one is also a great fit for me. I have a wonderful and caring supervisor and I have made some lasting friendships. When I accepted this job, I was aware of the sacrifice, but the perk outweighed the sacrifice. Life is like that for me. God will let me sit with the sacrifices for a time before showing me the perks. I have come to appreciate this process and I respect the wait now. I know that there will always be a rainbow after the storm and if I just hold on, I will feel the sunshine again. Some days will be better than others, but that is to be expected.

His Promise

But as for you, do not give up and be strong, for your work will be rewarded.

- 2 Chronicles 15:7

My Promise

I promise to be equally appreciative of the sacrifices and the perks.

Epilogue

My life has not been the easiest of journeys up to this point but I am grateful for my life experiences. I am who I am because of them. Here in 2020 I can say, without doubt, that I am healthy, wealthy and wise. I have come through on the other side of all of the hurt, pain and heartache. I have forgiven myself and I have forgiven everyone else. I am not exempt from being hurt again, but it will not break me. I have learned how to modify my expectation to meet people where they are, and that has tremendously helped with the amount of disappointment I experience.

My husband and I are stronger than ever. We've been together for ten years now. I am happy and healthy and whole. Jack is seven years old and he is a happy normal boy that loves his mom and dad. He is doing well in school and has friends running in and out of the house constantly, I love it. Mikey is inpatient at this time, we speak often and Quan, Jack and I visit him often. He seems happy and, believe it or not, he's the superstar of the facility. Mitch has not returned the calls of myself or the case workers that reached out to him.

AJ is raising her littles and I'm sure she is a great mother, doing the best that she can. My mother is doing well, according to my brother. My mom, AJ and I haven't spoken yet, but I'm sure when it's time, we will. I wish them the best and I'm sure they will be just fine.

My expectation of love is different now. It ebbs and flows, some days are better than others. Some days I show up and I give 100%, and other days it's much less. I understand the difference between abuse and misuse. I'm working on fostering healthy relationships and I thank God for my loved ones who have been a vital part of my healing.

My sister Nubi has been an intricate part in my process and we are still very close, we speak daily. She is a fiction writer, poet and an artist, in addition to being an awesome mom. My brother and I speak periodically, and he knows that I love and cherish him. He's a very funny comedian and has recently opened up for Gary Owens, Sommore and Tony Rock. I guess we both choose to make others feel good about themselves, and to laugh instead of cry.

Before I became a therapist, I realized I needed professional help and seeking therapy has helped me immensely, it was a driving force in wanting to make this my profession.

I am working on myself daily and look forward to sharing that with you in Part II.

His Promise

Praise the Lord, O my soul; all my inmost being, praise His holy name. Praise the Lord, O my soul, and forget not all His benefits – who forgives all your sins and heals all your diseases, who redeems your life from the pit and crowns you with love and compassion, who satisfies your desires with good things so that your youth is renewed like the eagles.

- Psalm 103:1-5

My Promise

I promise to allow God's plan to work in my life for the greater good of his glory.

***

Yushima Cherry Burks is a Motivational Speaker, Education and Empowerment Program Developer, and an MSW Therapist specialising in Mental Health and Substance Abuse. Follow her on...

Instagram: @yearofyushima

Twitter: @yearofyushima

For trainings, speaking engagements, or business visit
www.yearofyushima.com

www.yearofyushima.com

A publication by Tamarind Hill Press

www.tamarindhillpress.co.uk

**TAMARiND HiLL
.PRESS**

CPSIA information can be obtained
at www.ICGtesting.com
Printed in the USA
LVHW032104100121
675857LV00003B/149